"Life is all about relationships. This book is a must-read for those who want to lead in relationship building."

—C. William Pollard, chairman emeritus,
The ServiceMaster Company

"The journey that *Beyond Your Best* describes so well is truly an extraordinary experience, although not for the faint of heart. If we stay with the journey as the authors advise though, it takes us beyond our own minds and imaginations and leaves us astounded by grace. I would recommend this book for anyone who is sincerely attracted to the challenge of letting God take them to places they've never been before."

—Janet Hagberg, director, Silent Witness National Initiative,
and author, *Real Power* and *The Critical Journey*

"*Beyond Your Best* represents a ground-breaking blend of the technical and character aspects of life and leadership."

—Bill Hybels, chairman,
The Willow Creek Association

"This inspiring book is essential reading for those who seek to earn the respect of the emerging generation who hunger for leaders whose personal and professional lives are centered on character and dignity."

—Dick Capen, former U.S. ambassador to Spain;
chairman and publisher, *The Miami Herald*;
and author, *Finish Strong*

"Climbing the ladder of success is a driving passion for many in today's corporate America, but too often character is compromised on the way up. *Beyond Your Best* helped me think through both motives and means to true success."

—John Beckett, chief executive officer and chairman,
R. W. Beckett Corporation, and author,
*Loving Monday: Succeeding in Business
Without Selling Your Soul*

"*Beyond Your Best* shows how character is a lifelong building process between God and yourself that then translates into character and leadership."

—**Karl Eller, chief executive officer and chairman, The Eller Company**

"Fresh, introspective, noble—this book contrasts the conventional leadership climb to sacred truth, mature living, and selfless achievement. The authors deftly describe what it means to lead by example and answer one of life's greatest questions, 'Why do people follow?'"

—**William Boyajian, president,**
Gemological Institute of America

"No matter what your style, *Beyond Your Best* will make you reassess it. I hope that future leaders will adopt the important creative suggestions and insight in this book. A must-read for us all.'"

—**Wallace R. Hawley, founder, InterWest Partners;**
chairman, Center for Economic Policy Research,
Stanford University

"No topic is more timely for our culture than to learn how character and influence develop in relationships over a lifetime. *Beyond Your Best* shows us how to lay hold of it."

—**Larry Crabb, bestselling author; psychologist;**
founder, New Way Ministries

"This outstanding book of principles provides leaders with unusual how-to's and practical steps for developing character. *Beyond Your Best* is a remarkable look at how young leaders learn to serve others and how older leaders learn to reach their destiny."

—**Matthew Parker, president, Institute for**
Black Family Development

"This book is a profound and unique answer to the questions of our tumultuous society . . . uncompromising character development produces profound influence."

—**Naomi Rhode, past president, National Speakers Association,**
1997 Cavett winner

"Having spent several years on the staff at West Point contemplating the development of leaders of character, I find in *Beyond Your Best* a powerfully insightful, honest, and encouraging model for practice by leaders who are genuinely seeking to grow in character and reaching one's destiny."

—**Larry Donnithorne, author,** *The West Point Way of Leadership: From Fostering Principled Leadership to Practicing It*

"We live at a time in history when there is a pronounced vacuum in leaders of character and influence. Our need is for clear, inspiring, and above all timeless teaching on these subjects. *Beyond Your Best* powerfully provides us with all these and more."

—**Michael Card, best selling composer, author, teacher**

"Most people are familiar with challenges and risks. *Beyond Your Best* deals with the greatest risks any of us can face: humility, transparency, and sacrifice. This book will challenge you in unique ways and help you view your calling with a new perspective."

—**Jack Alexander, chief executive officer and chairman, Geronimo Holdings**

"*Beyond Your Best* fits in the fine lineage of Greenleaf's *Servant Leadership* and De Pree's *Leadership Is an Art*. A must-read for anyone who wonders about a deeper foundation and a higher pinnacle. Transcendent, transparent, and authentic."

—**Daryl C.F. Wilson, vice president of manufacturing, Zenon Environmental, Inc.**

"This profound and timely book teaches us how to live well and wisely. *Beyond Your Best* creatively shows us how to center our lives in unchanging principles that produce an enduring influence in all our relationships."

—**John R. Castle, Jr., executive vice president (retired), Electronic Data Systems**

"A fresh, revolutionary, look at relationships and destiny. This book will change you and the lives you touch."

—**Daniel Dominguez, CPA and partner, BDO Seidman, LLP**

"*Beyond Your Best* addresses the two most important questions anyone must answer if their lives and work are to have meaning: Who are you? And who cares? Character shapes cultures and culture nourishes character. Who you are makes a difference."

—Walter C. Wright, Jr., executive director,
De Pree Leadership Center

"In this remarkable and helpful book, the authors carefully and clearly help us to understand that people of influence are made, not necessarily born. Anyone who aspires to leadership—young or old, male or female— will be helped immensely by this significant publication."

—Ted W. Engstrom, president emeritus,
World Vision

"Great content. This book speaks of a character ladder that takes us beyond success to true significance . . . beyond achievement to leaving a legacy!"

—Merrill J. Oster, entrepreneur; author,
Vision-Driven Leadership

"As I read *Beyond Your Best* I had one reoccurring question, 'What would the impact be upon higher education in this country if every college president and student read and put into practice the principles of this book?' My answer to the question was, 'Let it begin with me!'"

—Jay A. Barber Jr., president,
Warner Pacific College

"*Beyond Your Best* is truly a profound book for anyone seeking their destiny. As a young leader of a family business, this book provided a roadmap (or ladder!) for me on how to lead from values and integrity."

—Louise Slater, chair of the board,
Consolidated Systems, Inc.

Other Books by Thrall, McNicol, and McElrath
The Ascent of a Leader

Beyond Your Best

Develop Your Relationships, Fulfill Your Destiny

Bill Thrall, Bruce McNicol,
Ken McElrath

JOSSEY-BASS
A Wiley Imprint
www.josseybass.com

Published by Jossey-Bass
A Wiley Imprint
989 Market Street, San Francisco, CA 94103-1741   www.josseybass.com

Jossey-Bass books and products are available through most bookstores.
To contact Jossey-Bass directly call our Customer Care Department within the U.S.
at 800-956-7739, outside the U.S. at 317-572-3986 or fax 317-572-4002.

Jossey-Bass also publishes its books in a variety of electronic formats. Some content
that appears in print may not be available in electronic books.

All Bible references, except as noted, are taken from *The Holy Bible, New International
Version.* Grand Rapids, Mich.: Zondervan, 1973 and 1978.

Chapter Three: Excerpt from *The Wisdom of the Sands* by Antoine de Saint-Exupery,
copyright © 1950 and renewed 1978 by Harcourt, Inc., reprinted by permission of the
publisher.

Chapter Five: *Soren Kierkegaard's Journals and Papers,* Vol. III, L-R, p. 535, serial number
3343. Edited and translated by Howard V. Hong and Edna H. Hong, assisted by Gregor
Malantschuk, Indiana University Press, Bloomington and Indianapolis.

Chapter Eight: "Healing Touch" written by Russ Taff, Tori Taff, and James Hollihan Jr.
Permission granted by Tori Taff Music and James Hollihan Music. Copyright © 1988.

Chapter Nine: From CALLINGS by Gregg Michael Levoy, copyright © 1997 by Gregg
Michael Levoy. Used by permission of Harmony Books, a division of Random House, Inc.

Chapter Ten: Excerpts from *Servant Leadership: A Journey into the Nature of Legitimate Power
and Greatness* by Robert K. Greenleaf, copyright © 1977. Used with permission of Paulist
Press. www.paulistpress.com

Library of Congress Cataloging-in-Publication Data
Thrall, Bill.
  Beyond your best: develop your relationships, fulfill your destiny /
Bill Thrall, Bruce McNicol, Ken McElrath.—1st ed.
    p. cm.
Includes bibliographical references.
  ISBN 0-7879-6762-9 (alk. paper)
  1. Success—Religious aspects—Christianity. I. McNicol, Bruce.
II. McElrath, Ken. III. Title.
BV4598.3.T47 2003
248.4—dc21   2002156252

Printed in the United States of America

FIRST EDITION
PB Printing   10 9 8 7 6 5 4 3 2 1

Contents

List of Figures

Dedicated to

Bill, Wende, and Joy
B.T.

Nicole, Chad, and Ryan
B.M.

Zach, Tommy, and Anne
K.M.

Preface

We owe a great debt to many people who have helped us experience the principles we have written about in this book. They have spoken truth to us when we needed to hear it. They have loved us despite our failures and frailties. They have helped us become far better husbands and fathers and leaders and people than we could have become on our own.

The stories shared in the following pages come from a variety of sources: personal experience, friends, biographies, cartoons, books, and comedians. We use our own first names when the stories come from our own lives. In an effort to protect the privacy of others, we have changed such identifying characteristics as name, location, and, in some instances, gender and occupation.

Special thanks to John Lynch, whose creative gifts will help you enjoy reading this book. Thanks to the board, staff, and advisory council of Leadership Catalyst, Inc., for their timeless encouragement. Thanks to Tom McGee and Mike Hamel, who assisted us in condensing and editing *Beyond Your Best,* and to Ellen Antill, Mark Carver, Amanda Smith, Wendy Hancock, David Sanford, and Vesta Walker, whose practical care, expertise, and affirmation have inspired us to do more than we thought possible. Thanks to the women and men of Open Door Fellowship for living these truths, to Leadership Network for championing this book before it was birthed, and to the board, staff, and urban leaders of Interest Associates and related organizations, who helped us gain many of these insights. The people of Jossey-Bass deserve rich praise for their publishing expertise and encouragement, as do the volunteer readers and researchers who contributed their insights to enrich this message. Finally, we would like to thank the many individuals who have given us permission to use their stories and U.S. Senator Jon Kyl, in particular, for his many helpful suggestions.

If you would like to know more about Leadership Catalyst, Inc., and its programs, please contact us at (888) 249–0700, or visit our Website, www.leadershipcatalyst.org.

Phoenix, Arizona
April 2003

BILL THRALL
BRUCE MCNICOL
KEN MCELRATH

Introduction

Imagine you were told that there existed a magical shiny blue pill. And if you took it, you'd awaken to find that you'd been given a rare, electrifying life—an incredible destiny, a sense of wild-eyed purpose unique to you. You'd retain your family and your friends but everything would be different. You'd be living with purpose, fulfillment, and a sense of deep significance. And your family and friends would be different, your relationships transformed. Your very presence would change theirs, and their changed lives would free yours. And near the end of your life, you'd look back and know that you really had made a difference. And you respond, "Oh, great! I picked up a fad diet book in the store by mistake. I wonder if I can still get my money back."

All right, erase the screen. Let's try again. Suppose somebody told you that locked inside you is this incredible person longing to get out, that your present talents and skills and training have taken you only so far. And you don't have the tools to go any further. And you respond, "Oh, great! I picked up a motivational self-help book in the store by mistake. I wonder if I can still get my money back."

OK, OK—one more try. Suppose you were told what you happen to already know: that something nags in you that says, "There's more to me, to the reason I've been put on this earth, and I don't know what it is. I know I have talents. I know I have stuff to offer. But I keep shooting myself in the foot. From the earliest time I can remember, I thought I was put on this earth to do something a whole lot more significant than what it seems like I'm doing right now. And it seemed like life would be more fulfilling than it is right now." And what if everything about that nagging thought is true?

So, now, what if you were told that the reason for this book is to help take you there, to that "whole lot more significant" land? Would you respond, "Oh, great! I just picked up a science fiction book in the store by mistake. I wonder if I can still get my money back"?

We hope not. Because the nagging dream you can't shake is not science fiction. It has been placed there by a God who made you—who has an incredible imagination and an even more incredible love for you.

We hope you'll read on. Many of us have had that nagging dream we can't shake. *Beyond Your Best*, dedicated to that dream, is written primarily for the nine people out of ten who believe in the existence of God. The principles we strive to live and teach here are for everyday people in everyday situations. They can be practiced by women and men in any relational context. Internalizing these truths will revolutionize your life and reshape how you relate to your world. And you don't have to be a genius to do this; even children can understand and apply these principles with success. A carpenter named Jesus once said, "Whoever becomes simple and elemental again, like this child, will rank high in God's kingdom," and "unless you accept God's kingdom in the simplicity of a child, you'll never get in."[1] Children understand the important things. The profound things. They don't bother picking truth or love apart like pulling the petals off a daisy until the beauty is gone. They simply accept truth and love with their hearts when they trust those who share it with them.

We want to encourage a type of childlike abandon as you read. Most children can switch gears rather quickly when something better comes along—leaving a toy behind to grasp the playful, inviting hand of a parent, for instance. Adults have a harder time with change, especially when it comes to letting go of patterns that have taken years to develop. But truth can reprogram our patterns for the better if we let it.

As you read the chapters that follow, ask yourself these questions: Will practicing these principles lead me to deeper, more loving relationships? Will applying these ideas inspire vision and hope in myself and those I influence? Will wearing the corrective lenses of trust and truth help me see who I really am and help me become all God intends me to be? We believe you will answer with a resounding "Yes!" to every question.

Chapter One

A Different Ladder
to Success

If you are to step out into the unknown, the place
to begin is with the exploration of the inner
territory.

                      —*James Kouzes and Barry Posner*

"Close the emergency doors!"

"They're already closed, Sir," the first officer replied to the captain, whom he would have addressed as E. J. under less stressful conditions.

"Send to the carpenter and tell him to sound the ship," responded the captain. But the carpenter had already perished in the attempt to make repairs. As the ship rapidly took on water, the instruments on the bridge clearly indicated their rapidly declining chances of survival.

While the steam sirens screamed in agony, the captain barked out orders. "Fire the rockets in case any ship can offer assistance. All hands on deck."

Less than a year earlier, the aging captain had tarnished his excellent record in an embarrassing collision with the HMS *Hawke*. Soon thereafter, he had damaged his newly repaired ship by sailing it over a submerged wreck. After fixing the broken propeller blade, the captain had determined to patch up his reputation and quell rumors of his deteriorating capacities. This voyage was to have done just that.

Sticking his head into the radio room, the captain shouted, "Send the call for assistance."

"What call shall I send?" the Marconi operator asked.

"The regulation international call for help. Just that," was Captain E. J.'s reply as he hurried away.

■ ■ ■

When the captain began this journey, he set a course and speed. He alone was responsible for the safety of the ship and its passengers. But the course he set took his ship into peril, even though he had been warned of the danger. And the speed he set ultimately determined its fate.

Although policy clearly dictated "moderate speed and maximum comfort," the captain had treated his new charge like a speedboat on open seas. He had thought that arriving ahead of schedule would go a long way in restoring his reputation. During the most dangerous part of the voyage, the confident captain had left his third-in-command on the bridge while he boasted to his dinner guests how the ship could be cut into three sections and each would float. He was certain the ship was unsinkable.

Little more than an hour after this boast, he issued his last command: "You have done your duty boys; now every man for himself."[1]

Captain Edward J. Smith perished with more than one thousand others in the icy Atlantic. His reputation was the least of his worries the night the *Titanic* went down.

Deeper Issues

Each of us leaves a legacy, an imprint on others. We want it to be good and strong, lasting and important. But early along the journey, we are confronted with an unrelenting daily howl from somewhere close by. It is the howl of expediency: *Get the thing done, at whatever cost, that makes you look good and brings maximum affirmation and acceptance.* It commands us to look only at the water a few feet ahead and ignore anything that isn't directly in our path; we must get what we think we must have. Like Captain Smith, we can become seduced to ignore submerged dangers until they rip out the bottom of our well-built plans. The deceptive, insidious crisis is this: we can ignore the warning signs for a while and still stay afloat. The metal-on-metal sounds of our undoing are hidden by the chop of our own propellers. What's worse, we will be applauded for the glossy appearance that expediency can bring. By the time the screaming grind of metal becomes so loud it can no longer be drowned out, the damage has already been done.

But early along the journey, we are confronted with an unrelenting daily howl from somewhere close by. It is the howl of expediency.

Here are the warning signs:

- Needing to impress others to feel OK about yourself
- Experiencing strained relationships
- Having a nagging sense of failure that no success can quell
- Becoming defensive at the slightest criticism
- Hiding behind your skills while fearing discovery of your true self
- Lacking the ability to trust God or others

Many of us set sail, intending to accomplish something significant, only to find that we have drifted off course. We become adrift in a boiling sea where change suddenly seems urgent and important, but we never get any closer to where we need to go. In shocked desperation, we begin to try anything and everything to get back on course. A new relationship, a different job, a better house, a nicer climate, better sound equipment, stronger will power, or the latest self-help program—all become, in turn, just one more heartbreaking, dry attempt at a course correction to bring us home. Like a ship without a GPS system or accurate navigational charts, we're making good time but have no idea where we're going.

The Climb of a Lifetime

Let's move this story to dry land. Have you ever climbed a ladder that was just too short to get you where you needed to go? And no matter how many times or how determinedly you climbed that ladder, it still didn't reach where you longed to go. This book is for those of us who have gotten tired of staring at the same brick wall from the top rung of a ladder that we have finally discovered is *just too short.*

Many of us set sail, intending to accomplish some-thing significant, only to find that we have drifted off course.

This book is an invitation to climb a different kind of ladder—a *really* different kind; it is as different as a bowl of broccoli cheese soup is from a present participle. This ladder goes *way up.* This ladder will leave you breathlessly charged as it carries you into a lifelong adventure of a realized destiny. This ladder has rungs that are strengthened in a newly rediscovered interdependency on God and others. There will be risks because you'll be up a lot higher than you were before. But you'll find you're no longer facing the risks alone, as you learn to help create and live within safe environments of trust. This environment becomes a blanket that envelops you and awakens and nurtures all the well-designed and perfectly planned purposes God has custom-designed for you.

Before you sign on for this ride, you should be warned. You will be challenged as to the way you've done life, done friendships, done *everything.* If you're like most of us, that'll be scary at times. You'll want to run back to the safe, normal, and predictable, even though it has never taken you where you longed to go. Such is the deceptive and manipulative nature of expediency. But you'll keep drinking in the sweet nectar of hope, and you'll keep tasting the promise of healthy purpose with others you are growing to love and trust. And what used to feel scary will suddenly feel very cool and very alive.

Of all the challenges in life, it is those we discover beneath the surface that will most affect the legacy of our influence. Read on. Embrace with courage and faith what is presented here. You won't regret it. For it will lead you to a place above and beyond your own, individual best.

Whose Best?

Some who read the title *Beyond Your Best* say to us, "That's impossible. You can't get any better than your best." It sounds like your old high school coach telling you to give 110 percent. Remember the first time you heard that? "But coach, I don't know if I can run 110 percent. It's just not possible, *is it?*" Then he gave you a stern look and made you run a bunch of laps. From then on you learned to ignore it as just one of those sayings coaches learn at a clinic somewhere.

But *this* title is no coach's motivational slogan. It is intentional and filled with truth: *the best you can offer will take you only so far.* For many of us, that has been our best for as long as we can remember. But there is a beautiful land beyond what you bring to the dance yourself. And you can get there. Take the "y" out of "your," and you will discover the foundation of this book. When life becomes defined by doing "our best," we believe you will fly by "your best" like it was standing still.

What you are now doing in your life may be excellent. But to rise above your individual best, you need a special kind of environment in which to live and work—an environment that nurtures a community that integrates your heart and hands, that nourishes your relationships with God and others around you. This kind of "best" is far more significant than your individual potential. It will exceed your individual goals. This kind of "best" will help you become more than you ever could become on your own. In this uplifting community, you actually become the kind of person others want to be around, even follow.

This wonderful reality is possible because this kind of environment is possible. *Beyond Your Best* will help you create and cultivate such a climate. Wherever this climate exists, it spreads a sense of safety and protection. Productivity and creativity blossom. Trust flourishes. Character matures.

Ah yes, *character*. That previously overlooked, highly talented, young, five-tool phenom in the six-player trade. Even the word can sound like a tired virtue illustrated in a Norman Rockwell painting. But unleashed, character changes homes, cities, and nations. When nurtured, it single-handedly makes the words of one with character trusted and powerful. It transforms relationships from self-protection into life-giving vulnerability.

Character—the inner world of motives and values that shapes our actions—is the ultimate determiner of the nature of our lives and influence. Character empowers our capacities while keeping them in check. It distinguishes those who use power well from those who abuse it. Character weaves integrity, honesty, and selfless service into the fabric of our families, organizations, and cultures.

In the past, some assumed the family would own the nurturing of character. But many families have forgotten how. Others thought the church would shoulder the role. But asking who owns the nurturing of character begs a fundamental question: Where does God come in? Good question.

Try this on: We believe there is a God who is intimately aware of and involved in our lives. The authors of this book each have a distinctly Christian faith, rooted in a biblical conviction of grace, coupled with truth. We are convinced that the principles and processes flowing out of grace will radically transform *anyone* who wants them.

The Value of "Our Best"

This is a great book for managers, but it's not about management. It's a helpful book on leadership, but it's not simply for leaders. Families will profoundly benefit from what's written here, but we aren't guaranteeing perfect marriages or trouble-free children. It's an incredibly important book for those soon to graduate from college, but it won't help much on a Botany final. What we are providing is practical help for ordinary people who want to develop extraordinary lives. We invite you to explore these principles, relationships, and environments with us, not in theory alone but in practice. At the end of each chapter, we provide some strategic key issues and questions. This isn't homework. It is life work. Open your heart and grapple with each of them. Take time with this book. Don't skim. You can't process the truths offered here in a lunch break. Give yourself this gift. The train doesn't come by this stop every day.

Grabbing Hold

- In the course you have set for your life, how are you providing for the safety of those you influence?
- As you look over your shoulder, who is in the wake of your influence and how are they doing?

Chapter Two

Perils of the
Short Ladder

It is sometimes frightening to observe the success
which comes even to the outlaw with a polished
technique. But I believe we must reckon with
character in the end, for it is as potent a force in
world conflict as it is in our own domestic affairs.
It strikes the last blow in any battle.

—*Philip D. Reed*

The divorce papers had been served. After many years of marriage, Jim's wife now despised him. He sat alone in the room of an out-of-the-way hotel, ashamed and distraught at the course his life had taken. Even his children held him in contempt. They would all be glad when he was finally gone.

Although he was a multimillionaire, Jim felt worthless. At the peak of his career, despair overwhelmed him. He had spent his entire life pursuing what he wanted. But tonight, as he sat in that cheap hotel counting the cost, he knew he had thrown away what he truly needed more than anything. His choices had destroyed all the significant relationships in his life. He thought it would be easier to simply end it all than to look into the mirror in that dim bathroom and face the horror of his failure in the face. Just a few pills. Just one pull of the trigger. . . .

■ ■ ■

How did Jim get to such a place? How does anyone so strong and alive, so successful-looking on the surface, end up in that hotel, in a terrifying depth of despair? This scene is played out more often than you might think.

Where does it start? It starts usually way back, undetected. It often starts the first time false appearances to gain acceptance win out over the truthful presentation of who we are.

Our friend and colleague John Lynch wanted so much to be popular and accepted, as he sat in his second-grade class at Baldy View elementary school. The World Series was on the radio. Back in 1961, teachers often let the games be broadcast in their entirety during class. There was a pinch-hitter for the Pirates at that time named Jerry Lynch. He was a great pinch-hitter. And he was, on this particular day, the hero of the game. Somewhere in about the eighth inning, after Jerry Lynch hit a pinch-hit home run to send the Pirates into the lead, John suddenly found himself blurting out, *"You know, he's my cousin."* There, he said it. It wasn't true, but hey, they *did* both have the same last name. Besides, who would ever know? And maybe this would be the ticket to lasting acceptance and love. Immediately, John was the center of attention. It was the talk of Baldy View throughout the series.

Most second-graders had little reason to doubt the claim. And John, basking in his new-found celebrity, didn't let it drop there. *"I think I might even be able to get a few tickets for the last couple games of the series."* Eventually, a fellow student's big brother figured out that for John to be the player's cousin, his mom would have had to deliver him at around age eight. The embarrassing issue was swept under the rug by a caring teacher, but the damage had been done. The acclaim he received—the instant acceptance—grooved a pattern that kept John inventing manufactured appearances even into adulthood. That pattern is not easily broken.

John's story is not the exception. At about the same age, Bruce also learned how to hide. While standing in the lunch line one day, he suddenly decided to drop out, giving up his coveted place near the front. The lady behind the counter gave him a puzzled look. A couple of his friends asked him where he was going. Bruce replied, "I'm not really hungry."

In fact, Bruce had just swallowed his lunch money! He had an odd habit of keeping his lunch money safe by putting it in his mouth; somewhere in line, he lost his focus and swallowed it. So he thought, "Oh boy, this can't be good. What am I gonna say to the lady at the cash register? 'Hey, I just swallowed my lunch money. It's in there, I promise.'" Bruce couldn't bring himself to admit his mistake to anyone. Having no lunch seemed better than being humiliated in public by the older kids ("Hey, there he is! That's the kid who carries lunch money in his mouth! Hey, kid, you got change for a dollar in there?"). They could be cruel. So he hid the real issues and tried to cover up, going hungry in order to save face. And he succeeded.

Bruce's predicament may seem silly or even irrelevant, but don't miss this point: *grown-ups, even those in the most significant roles, make the same kind of choices each day.* We hide our motives, weaknesses, habits, fears, and agendas, hoping that others will buy the image of confidence and success we are trying to project.

Latent "Deception Chips"

Thousands of young girls and boys possess latent "deception chips" just like John's and Bruce's. Drop them into environments where "what they do" becomes more important than "who they are becoming," and the deception chip automatically activates. First-graders quickly learn that there are important measurements of their worth, value, and acceptance going on all the time:

- Needing to outperform others and impress the teacher
- Wearing the right hair styles and cool clothes
- Staying one-up in the insult game
- Getting invited into the right peer group
- Not getting caught putting your lunch money in your mouth

As we grow older, the measurements and comparisons get more sophisticated:

- Body size and shape
- The number of zeros on our paycheck
- The car we drive
- Our golf handicap or the largest bass we've caught
- The neighborhood we live in
- Our children's grades and athletic skill

When our classrooms, homes, workplaces, and boardrooms become sufficiently competitive, the cost of nonconformity becomes too high. So we begin to become skillful at hiding parts of who we are. Even our recreation can become a driven effort to prove significance instead of a source of relaxation and rejuvenation. Such a performance-driven culture drains our spirits, minds, and bodies. Whether we are professional athletes, students, entrepreneurs, or forklift operators, our influence must rest on something more stable than our latest score, grade, profit-and-loss statement, or pay raise. We must be developing our "inner life" or our "outer world" will eventually crush us like empty pop cans.

Seeds of Destiny

Competing with all that noise is an equally strong desire to have our lives count. We want to have the ability to change ourselves and our environments for the better, to set things right, to be the kind of men and women others look up to. But many of us have almost no clue how to get there.

Deep inside each soul, God sows a seed of destiny. The seed starts out small—so small it may go unnoticed or ignored for years. But it is there, and because it is from God there is something more to our lives than meets the eye. Just as a vine bears its flowers and then its fruit, so our seed is designed to unfold, revealing more and more of God's intended plan and purpose for our lives—our destiny.

God uses every life experience, both good and bad, to mold and shape us uniquely toward specific purposes and goals for our lives.

Although God masterfully knits the strands together, we share responsibility in the process of weaving our destiny. We choose which threads to pull, which colors to highlight. Each decision is made in response to what we believe about ourselves and our world. Each action reveals the fabric of our faith. Together, with God, we fashion the tapestry that is our destiny and determine the influence we will have on our world. Wow! If that's true, then we're not automatons reacting to a predetermined script but vital partners with the God who made our very soul. Well, laddie, that ramps up the stakes a bit, doesn't it?

Unlikely Influencers

Some people make good choices early, and consequently their lives draw the praise and trust of others. They experience a rich, full joy in whatever they are given to do. Sometimes they influence a family in a profound way. Often they develop broad spheres of public influence; examples are people like George Washington, Mother Teresa, Billy Graham, and Booker T. Washington. Most of these great leaders never set out to be great; they simply had leadership thrust upon them. The tongue-in-cheek historian Dave Barry writes that our first president "was chosen to represent Virginia at the Continental Congress, a group of colonists who wanted to revolt against the King because he made them wear wigs and tights. They chose Washington to lead their army because he was strong and brave and not in the room at the time."[1]

Those who make it into the history books and the newspapers are inspiring to the rest of us. However, the most influential people of all time remain unknown, except to those whose lives they have affected. These are the teachers, scout leaders, parents, coaches, bosses, coworkers, or friends whose kindness, encouragement, and example have helped others move toward their destiny.

Stop there for a moment. We don't usually value ideas like this, do we? We think, "Yeah, right. Give me fame, public importance, and notoriety any day. Those are the heavy hitters. Those are the ones who get talked about. Those are the world shapers." We're cynical. We suspect we're being thrown a bone by people who don't really believe what they're saying any more than we do. We're being told what we're doing is significant, though largely unnoticed? Does that make sense? We think not. We want highly visible adulation—*and* significance.

Let's think about that view of significance for a moment. Read through this "quiz."[2] You don't have to answer each question. The purpose of the list will become evident as you read:

1. Name the five wealthiest people in the world.
2. Name the last five Heisman trophy winners.
3. Name the last five winners of the Miss America contest.
4. Name ten people who have won the Nobel or Pulitzer Prize.
5. Name the last half-dozen Academy Award winners for best actor and actress.
6. Name the last decade's worth of World Series winners.

Now consider a very different list:

1. List a few teachers who aided your journey through school.
2. Name three friends who've helped you through a difficult time.
3. Name five people who have taught you something worth-while.
4. Think of a few people who have made you feel appreciated and special.
5. Think of five people you enjoy spending time with.
6. Name half a dozen heroes whose stories have inspired you.

The lesson of the quiz is pretty obvious: *what we have longed for may not get us what we wanted, and what we didn't want may actually be giving us what we long for.* Those who have had an impact on our lives, who have made a difference to us, whose accomplishments stick in our soul are not the wealthy, the honored, the famous, the beautiful, the brilliant, the promoted, the publicized, the talented, the idolized, the record-setters. They are the ordinary, daily people who have, up-close, surrounded you with love, support, truth, and grace as you've run your race. Key relationships are so designed that they would have inordinate influence and significance in your life, more than the most famous, wealthy, or talented ever could from a distance.

There is an odd irony to the way life is designed. If I pursue power, if I pursue public acclaim, the pursuit itself will change the very fiber of who I am. So when and if I finally gain that acclaim and exaltation, the experience will be robbed of its delight. A desperate race begins, like a greyhound chasing a plastic rabbit, with the rate of return diminishing at every turn.

If I pursue exaltation, if I pursue public acclaim, the pursuit itself will change the very fiber of who I am.

However, if I pursue God's plan, if I pursue character, if I climb onto a longer ladder, I *will* discover my destiny and embrace the dream God has planted inside me. This enjoyment is not self-serving or vain. It is the delight of watching God release his intentions through my very life.

You think, almost out loud, "If I could believe that, everything in my life would change!" Well, read on friend. This is about to get fun.

The Ladder of Life

During the summers of his university days, Bruce worked for an electrical contractor. Several journeymen enjoyed the twisted thrill of testing his rookie mettle, exposing him to extreme heights, dark tunnels, and shocking experiments. One day, they asked Bruce to climb a too-old ladder truck to install some too-high lights.

Climbing the first extension was no problem. But as he continued onto the next extension, connections (and knees) began to wobble. Just before Bruce reached the final rung, the ladder hooks malfunctioned and the extensions collapsed; he plummeted earthward. Bruce's rapid descent stopped just ten feet short of the ground as the foot of the uppermost extension slammed into the bed of the truck. He barely hung on to an upper rung, preventing serious injury. He escaped with a few hand injuries and the memory of another round of veteran-tough laughter from the electrical pros.

Many of us discover that our lives are like climbing that ladder— a challenging and unpredictable ascent, often stable at the base and shaky at the top. From the bottom, life higher up looks alluring, and many attack the ladder with gusto for this reason, confident they possess what it takes to reach the top. They seek to rise above and dominate others by climbing a ladder of self-improvement we call the capacity ladder.

The Capacity Ladder

Each of us has the opportunity to make use of ladders to scale our walls. The ladder most are familiar with is one we call the capacity ladder. Although they come in diverse and sometimes elaborate forms, each ladder has the same four basic rungs.

The ascent up the capacity ladder begins with the first rung: *discover what I can do* (see Figure 2.1). For instance, when Ken was young, a favorite aunt pointed out and encouraged his ability to draw, and a high school teacher helped him discover his knack for writing. Several of Bill's teachers encouraged his gifts in math and critical thinking. Bruce's entrepreneurial skills expressed themselves early on when he started carnivals, pageants, and student revenue programs. In addition to specific skills, our "what-I-can-do inven-

Figure 2.1. The Rungs of the Capacity Ladder

tory" may include natural leadership inclinations such as a winsome personality, a dynamic influence, or an ability to craft a compelling vision or to persuade.

Moving up to the second rung—*develop my capacities*—grants more influence through our abilities. At this level, we sharpen our talents and gifts. We begin to rely on abilities and success as the source of significance. We gain self-confidence, and others are attracted to us because of what we can do well.

The successful scaling of the first two rungs attracts the attention of friends, executives, administrators, professors, and group members or leaders who recognize our strengths and abilities. This attention catapults us to the third rung—*acquire title or position*—where we believe others will look up to us, and our influence will grow if we keep performing well. This step up leads naturally to the fourth and final rung: *attain individual potential*. From below, the top rung of the capacity ladder looks great—honor, glory, respect, and power—becoming a person who is seen as successful, having great influence on others.

Is there anything wrong with the rungs on the capacity ladder? Not at all. The desire to face greater challenges and fulfill our potential is a natural part of being human. As creatures designed in God's image, we have an inborn impulse to better our lives, do meaningful things, and bring order to our world. When we deny this drive, we become something less than God intended. From the very beginning, God gave humanity the task of tending a garden and then expanded that stewardship to include caring for the world. Each of us is created with capacities intended for good.[3] But the capacity ladder is not sufficient. It can't support the deepest longing, which is to be a worthwhile person with an enduring legacy.

Lonely at the Top

Someone once said, "It's lonely at the top, but you eat better." After achieving a measure of success and influence, many begin to reflect on how they got to the top of the capacity ladder. Because we want to stay there, we keep our focus on what people told us worked in getting us there. This is where it's easy to start resembling a chameleon. "What do they want me to look like? What keeps me in this place? What appearance do I put on to make sure I stay here?" Most of us are keenly aware of our faults and weaknesses. We fear that if others knew us as we really are, they would reject us. So at the top of the capacity ladder, we feel trapped, hiding our true self behind the facade we have created out of our strengths and abilities. But now there is so much to lose, so much risk, that even if we admit to ourselves that something isn't right, the pressure to maintain position, authority, or role is so strong I am forced to put away such thoughts and begin to hide even better.

In environments where the definition of success does not include healthy relationships and character traits like honesty and integrity, some may accomplish much but wound so many along the way that no one trusts them anymore. Like escaped convicts, they scurry from one hiding place to another, just beyond the teeth of the pursuing hounds. The longer they run from the truth within, the more energy they expend in the attempt to escape themselves and those they have hurt. They fear facing the deeper issues, so their relationships and influence remain stunted, supported only by the capacity ladder.

Have you ever known someone like this? Someone who has refused to acknowledge and address the cracks in his heart? Someone who is reaping the benefits of having attained individual accomplishments? Talent, gifts, and performance shine in these people. But immature character tarnishes their influence. Something is toxically wrong within.

Usually it is relational problems that expose this character immaturity. When people with undeveloped character depend only on the capacity ladder, their actions have a negative impact on those around them. Friendships become fragmented and superficial. Instead of admitting their mistakes, they may try to cover them up, becoming even more isolated. As Blaise Pascal perceptively observed, "Truly it is an evil to be full of faults, but it is a still greater evil to be full of them and to be unwilling to recognize them."[4] This evil leads to the distortion of undervaluing others and overvaluing themselves, wreaking havoc in relationships.

> *Truly it is an evil to be full of faults, but it is a still greater evil to be full of them and to be unwilling to recognize them.*
>
> —BLAISE PASCAL

Redefining Success

Those who trust and follow such leaders eventually pay for their trust, sometimes with tragic results. Why do they follow? Because followers see the strength of personality (rung one), benefit from the leader's developed gifts (rung two), place confidence in the leader's office or position (rung three), and assume . . . what? They assume the leader's emotional, spiritual, and relational maturity. What's almost as bad, the followers' misplaced trust tempts the leader to further duplicity and hiddenness. The capacity ladder, when promoted and honored by itself, is breaking down in companies, families, ministries, and schools all over the world. For the failed, compromised, entrusted, hidden, desperate climber of only the capacity ladder, no amount of money, power, praise, or authority can any longer define success. There is a sudden dawning of awareness that what they thought was success *isn't*, and what success *is* requires a ladder they have no idea how to find, buy, or climb. That dawning is life's critical crossroads. Standing in front of it, we will either fall into passive despair, redouble our efforts, or, just maybe, for the first time, learn how to live.

Starting Over

For some, a fall from the top exposes their inner failures; for others, staying at the top *is* their failure. For the latter group, failure means living with an intimate awareness of an inner cancer eating away at their very being, reminding them daily that something is wrong. In such cases, a fall may come as a relief, giving the opportunity for fresh start. That's what happened to Jim, the man whose story began this chapter.

Eight years after the scene in the hotel, Jim took the podium at a business luncheon. He told stories of his past pursuits and his rise to power. He captured everyone's attention when he told of selling his privately owned company for $400 million. But the real story began as he described the ultimate impact of his past choices, culminating that night when he hid in the hotel room, contemplating suicide.

Something began to die that night: a cancer deep inside his heart. His dogged pursuit of power suffered a lethal dose of radiation, and the stranglehold that money had on his life began to loosen. Jim's influence didn't decrease after his experience; it began to expand. The financial rewards of his business blossomed. But instead of becoming a slave to his increased success, he began to give of himself and his money in increasing measure to worthy causes. Jim finished his speech by challenging other businesspeople to do the same.

Jim had been influential from his youth. But now his influence had been altered in a way that benefited others while nourishing his own heart and soul. He had found a different path. Where? And how? What made the difference in his character, relationships, and therefore his influence? The answer didn't come from his abilities and capacities, his position of power and authority. In fact, his bondage to these very things almost destroyed him before he reevaluated and altered his path.

This different path involves a time-tested process of intentionally ascending a different kind of ladder—a ladder that can actually prevent you from falling. We hope many reading this book have a chance to begin *intentionally* building this second ladder before going too far in life's journey. If you're on the bottom rungs of the ladder and you fall, it doesn't hurt as much. This ladder leads to influence, too. It also produces results. But of a very different nature.

Grabbing Hold

- Who benefits from your success?
- In setting direction, are you reacting to circumstances or acting on convictions?
- If climbing the capacity ladder does not fulfill you, what will?
- What benefits have you gained from those who most influenced you?

Chapter Three

Environments That Support and Empower

If you want to build a ship, don't drum up the men
to gather wood, divide the work, and give orders.
Instead, teach them to yearn for the vast and
endless sea.

—*Antoine de Saint-Exupéry*

With a knock at the front door and an invitation for the visitor to enter, the door flew open. The bishop, his sister, and the housekeeper, Madame Magloire, were stunned by the appearance of a menacing figure lurking in the doorway. He announced himself as Jean Valjean and gruffly explained that he was a convict who had been a galley slave for nineteen years. Jean Valjean had been walking for four days traveling to Pontarlier, and he needed shelter and some food. The bishop calmly instructed Madame Magloire to add another plate to the dinner table.

Jean Valjean was taken aback by the generous invitation of the bishop and guessed the bishop must not have understood that he was a dangerous criminal. With this, he pulled his yellow passport from his pocket and insisted the bishop read about the five years he had spent in the galleys for burglary and an additional fourteen years for multiple attempts to escape. Previously, whenever he would present his yellow passport indicating that he was a liberated convict, he had been refused shelter or food. Jean Valjean told the bishop that he had money and would simply like some food to eat and, perhaps, a place to sleep in the stable. Amazingly, the bishop invited him in and asked Madame Magloire to prepare a bed inside the house for Jean Valjean. That night a stunned Valjean joined the unlikeliest of companions for dinner and a night of comfort in the home of the kind bishop.

During the night Valjean awoke, struggling with the demons of his past. Overcome by his sense of failure, he decided his life was as worthless as the yellow passport he carried in his pocket. In his despair, deciding to return to the only life he knew, he arose, gathered his knapsack, and prepared to leave the bishop's home. First, Valjean went to the bishop's cupboard, ready to break open the lock if necessary. To his surprise the cupboard was unlocked and the key lay inside. Quickly, he stuffed the bishop's silver plates into his knapsack and fled the home, running through the garden and escaping over the fence.

The next morning, after the housekeeper found Valjean and the silver missing, she alerted the bishop. Expecting the bishop to be as angry as she, Madame Magloire was stunned at the bishop's explanation that he should have given the silver to the poor long ago and that obviously this man was poor and needed it more than the bishop's household.

As they sat down at the table for breakfast, a familiar figure appeared. Following an abrupt knock at the door, Valjean again entered the home, but this time in the custody of three fierce gendarmes. The captain of the gendarmes approached the bishop, who rose and walked briskly toward the group of men. He went straight to Jean Valjean. A sullen Valjean was ready for a reprimand but was incredulous as the bishop said to him, "Ah, there you are! I am glad to see you. But, I gave you the candlesticks also, which are silver like the rest, and would bring two hundred francs. Why did you not take them along with your plates?" At the explanation of the bishop the confused gendarmes released Valjean and left the home.

As the bishop handed the candlesticks to Jean Valjean, Valjean was astounded by the bishop's grace. "Jean Valjean, my brother, you belong no longer to evil, but to good. It is your soul that I am buying for you. I withdraw it from dark thoughts and from the spirit of perdition, and I give it to God!"

■ ■ ■

Perhaps no one has better captured the spirit of grace than Victor Hugo in his opening scene of *Les Miserables*.[1] Grace broke into Jean Valjean's life through simple acts of unexpected kindness, transforming him and spreading into the lives of the desperate people whom God brought into the life of the former convict.

Our hearts leap when we hear stories like this; something quickens deep within. We want to experience this kind of life, this kind of *grace*. We also want to become the kind of person who, like the bishop, shares surprising grace with others. But we wonder, How could that ever happen to me? How do I learn to receive the surprising grace that Jean Valjean stumbled into? How do I learn to give it as the bishop did? How could I learn to live in a way that releases grace in me to become all God intends? How do I develop the kind of character that spreads grace, bringing out the best in others?

Environments of Grace

Grace. The word carries on its shoulders all we hope could be true. It's the free lunch nobody's supposed to get. It's the "get out of jail free" card. When used by God toward humans, it conveys the unspeakable truth that we are finally off the hook we placed ourselves on. *Really* off the hook. It means we are able to have a relationship with God without looking over our shoulders or waiting for the next shoe to drop. It is undeserved, unending, unexplainable, unfeasible, unearned, unwavering, inexhaustible love to the unlovely. It pierces into our deepest shame, failure, and abandoned fear to declare, "I know, and I'm not leaving. I'm crazy about you."

In *Traveling Mercies*, Anne Lamott beautifully describes grace toward us.

> It is unearned love—the love that goes before, that greets us on the way. It's the help you receive when you have no bright ideas left, when you are empty and desperate and have discovered that your best thinking and most charming charm have failed you. Grace is the light or electricity or juice or breeze that takes you from that isolated place and puts you with others who are as startled and embarrassed and eventually grateful as you are to be there.[2]

It is almost too good to be true. *Almost*. But it is true. And when it captures us, it reshapes us.

You, who believe and start to live in the environment of grace, are one of the beautiful ones, the free ones, the giving ones. You walk around shaking your head, the way you would a week after being told you'd won the Irish Sweepstakes. It catches you off-guard again for the umpteenth time. It really happened to *you!* Somewhere, in the deepest part of us, grace is the way we thought it should be. But somewhere between not being picked on the playground and being rejected in a job, a marriage, or a friendship, we stopped believing. Like Wendy in Peter Pan, we stopped believing there was a never-never-land available here and now and instead learned to settle for the cold winter of a coal-blackened city, where deadlines and products determine worth.

As we relate to each other, grace offers unmerited concern and favor to each other. Like the bishop, we may even turn our most treasured possessions over to the likes of Jean Valjean—vagrant convicts who cheat us, steal from us, and lie to us. Grace means we treat each other better than we expect to be treated. Grace transcends justice. We meet a need expecting nothing in return. We forgive. We release.

Grace means we pay back insults with love, as the reformed Valjean did when he took in a dying prostitute who had spat in his face, then went further by promising to care for her orphaned daughter, Cosette.

Grace begets grace. Trace an act of grace back to its roots, and you will find its ultimate source is God. Follow an act of grace to its conclusion, and you will find that eventually it leads people to God's presence. For instance, the bishop received grace from God and passed it on to Valjean. As a result, Valjean soon found God and received his grace directly. He then passed it on to a desperate woman trapped in prostitution. The woman soon found God. The unmerited favor of God, when transferred through surprising acts of human kindness, can transform even the most hardened hearts.

Now here's the bizarre, inexplicable part of the story. We may understand grace as how God would like us to know him. We may even live in that truth for ourselves. But somehow it doesn't translate for us to relationships. We can't make the application. It's like the guy who drops his wallet one evening on a street corner. A friend passes by and asks, "What are you doing?" "I'm looking for the wallet I lost on the other side of the street." Incredulous, his friend asks, "If you lost it over there, why are you looking over here?" "Oh, the light's better over here." He knows he's lost a wallet and he knows he needs light. But he's missing the application of the facts to the situation.

We're the same with grace. We don't seem to be able to make the application. We personally may want to exhibit graciousness, but the thought of an environment run on the basis of grace sounds as odd to us as a pair of shorts made out of Velveeta cheese. We've seen grace. But when we get back inside and sit down to the daily life we've chosen, we presume we will receive something very much unlike grace.

Somehow we have convinced ourselves that grace does not work in groups. Instead, we resort to the ugly monsters *we* fear most to get things done. Control works. Leverage works. Threatening works. Fear works. Or does it?

Powerful Environments

There are wonderful examples of environments of grace, and anyone who has tasted one hungers for more. Most of us know an environment of grace when we see or feel it. You walk into a room where it exists, and it's almost as if you can feel the accepting safety. The results are as obvious as they are rare: people feel secure, they grow up, they trust each other, they're not looking over their shoulder, they live authentically, they celebrate each other, they laugh a lot, they produce better. For example, wherever Dr. Gerald May of the Shalem Institute finds communities where people successfully combat destructive addictions, he feels such an environment. "Its power includes not just love that comes from people and through people, but love that pours forth among people, as if through the very spaces between one person and the next. Just to be in such an atmosphere is to be bathed in healing power."[3]

In such an environment, people feel empowered. They sense that who they are is OK, even though they know greater things are expected from them. They perceive the freedom to make important contributions, even when their suggestions require significant changes or their questions test long-held assumptions. They discern a positive spirit that acts as a catalyst in their soul, giving them a sense of hope that "here is a place where I belong." This is home.

Taking Hold of the Rails

Environments of grace are built with the aid of a different kind of ladder. This ladder can be distinguished from the capacity ladder in a number of ways.

First of all, it has more rungs—five instead of four—so it's naturally longer. In the chapters that follow, we will discuss each of these rungs in detail. This ladder could go by a number of names because it produces a multitude of powerful benefits. It could be called the ladder of promise, the ladder of grace, the ladder of healthy relationships, or even the ladder of destiny. Because the rungs represent principles that can help people intentionally develop character, we will call it the character ladder.

Second, the character ladder requires a great deal more personal and relational investment to master than its shorter counterpart—investments that pay rich dividends.

Third, the character ladder has longer and stronger rails. Here the differences between the character and capacity ladders begin to be keenly felt. On both ladders, one rail represents environment and the other represents relationships. Environment and relationships are two sturdy rails on the same ladder. Developing healthy relationships in an unhealthy environment is nearly impossible, as is constructing a positive environment with a group of negative people (see Figure 3.1).

Figure 3.1. The Rails of the Character Ladder

*An environment
of grace works
side by side with
relationships of trust
to create cultures
in which creativity,
hope, and other
positive outcomes
emerge.*

An environment of grace works side by side with relationships of trust to create cultures in which creativity, hope, and other positive outcomes emerge. Leadership sage Chris Argyris confirms that "without interpersonal competence or a 'psychologically safe' environment, the organization is a breeding ground for mistrust, inter-group conflict, rigidity and so on, which lead to a decrease in organizational success in problem solving."[4] This is true not only for business environments but for homes, schools, churches, and social organizations. Safe environments produce confident, secure people who help others feel safe enough to deal with the deeper issues of character.

The Penalties of Ungrace

Just as the outcomes of an environment of grace can be clearly seen, so can those of an environment lacking grace, or as the writer Philip Yancey calls it, *ungrace*. Argyris points out some of these ungracious outcomes: mistrust, conflict, rigidity, and decreased problem-solving abilities, along with a dozen others. In an atmosphere of ungrace, favor and love must be earned. When humans feel they cannot earn favor or love without meeting a too-high standard, they lose hope. Or they pretend they have no frailties or weaknesses. At home, work, school, and church, we build facades to protect our vulnerable inner selves. We use walls and masks to present the right image to others and deceive ourselves into thinking we don't have to deal with what we have successfully hidden.

Oddly enough, the very places we would expect to find grace many times reflect it the least. Some churches and religious organizations manufacture the worst kind of capacity ladders by requiring strict adherence by their people to a set of do's and don'ts in order to be accepted or respected.

Ungrace in the church is often lampooned by the media, and nowhere with more biting wit than on Sunday evenings with "The Simpsons." Homer and his family and neighbors attend the First Church of Springfield. "In front of the main entrance of the contemporary structure," writes Mark Pinsky in *The Gospel According to the Simpsons*,

> is a marquee that changes weekly, with black letters on a white background. The sign features a variety of messages, ranging from half-hearted and self-conscious efforts to be hip . . . to those more in keeping with the pastor's view of theology and the role of the church. The more illustrative include: "Sunday, the Miracle of Shame," "No Shirt, No Shoes, No Salvation," and "Private Wedding: Please Worship Elsewhere."[5]

Humor is most effective when it is wrapped around a kernel of truth. However, faith communities also have the greatest potential to be the most profound examples of enclaves of grace.

When our friend Wendy first experienced an environment of grace, she didn't enjoy it very much. As a successful stockbroker eyeing a political career, Wendy had enjoyed a charmed life as the well-loved, well-educated, well-adjusted child of a wonderfully functional family. One Sunday, at the suggestion of her husband, Wendy visited a new church. At least that's what her husband called it.

To Wendy, a bunch of people wearing everything from suits to shorts and sandals, a preacher wearing Levi's and sneakers, and a "choir" consisting of (in her words) "a four-piece rock band with four 'back-up chicks'" did not seem anything like a real church. What was worse, she embarrassed herself by laughing out loud with everyone else during the preacher's sermon. But by the time the sermon ended, tears streaked her cheeks. Something deep inside her had been touched.

She tried to bolt for the car as soon as the service ended but was stopped by an old high school friend who used to be the consummate bad boy. He greeted her with a broad smile and said, "Isn't this place great?"

"What happened to *him?*" she wondered as she pressed on to the parking lot. In the car, her husband wanted to know what she thought of the place. "I hated it!" Wendy replied.

"I thought so," he said, "but would you consider giving it another try?"

"I can't believe I'm saying this," Wendy answered, "but I think we have to go back. I don't know why, but I felt something in there that I've never felt before. I don't want to, but I know I have to go back."

Wendy did go back. Several years earlier, Wendy's husband had contracted cancer. Then her first-born daughter almost died from a severe neurological illness. Shortly after settling into the church, Wendy's doctors diagnosed a life-threatening complication during her third pregnancy—life-threatening for her and the baby. Things seemed to be crumbling all around her. What happened to that perfect, predictable, and productive life?

Wendy and her family needed help. The environment at that church gave her the strength she needed to risk asking for, and receiving, that help. Because she felt unmerited favor, she could openly ask hard questions about suffering without fear of belittlement. Because she found safety, she could express her sorrow and grief. In this environment, she could risk admitting her needs, without fearing loss of respect for her abilities and potential. The people at the church responded to her with listening ears and helping hands. Please don't miss this point: *it was the environment that melted away Wendy's resistance to receiving the care of others*. The fact that she found such a climate at a church is not the point. The truth is, far too few churches possess such an environment, regardless of their stated theological commitments to grace.

Surprising Grace Places

Environments of grace can also appear in the most unlikely places, like Silicon Valley. Rick McEachern, former senior marketing manager at Apple Computer, suggests that the environment "set the tone" for Apple's return to fiscal health and prominence in the computing world of the late nineties. One of the first things Steve Jobs did was to consolidate staff from a variety of scattered buildings into a newly constructed campus. On this campus, you can go to work in a suit or jeans. You can wear your hair long or shave it off. You can hold a meeting in a coffee bar, a gymnasium, or a comfy conference room full of toys. In short, you are encouraged to be yourself. In addition, you are always part of a team that cannot accomplish its goal without you.[6] We need an environment where we sense the freedom to be who we are, within boundaries framed by values and a common goal. We need to feel we are safe and supported as whole people who have significant things to contribute, despite our differences.

Of course, you may say, Jobs is no ordinary person, and he was handed an extraordinary opportunity few of us will ever encounter. Maybe. But the same principles apply in the most humble circumstances. We have the opportunity each day to create an atmosphere of care and concern where hope and vision can flourish. But tough choices need to be made and hard questions asked. Can we set aside a solely personal agenda to embrace one that benefits others? Can we accept people who look, act, and even believe differently from us if we know it will release their potential? Can we declare our own strengths, admit our own frailties, and receive the strengths of others despite their weaknesses?

How can we open ourselves up to the possibilities of an environment of grace when we may not be experiencing an environment of grace ourselves? We may say, "It's just not that simple!"

Actually, it is that simple. At home, work, school, or at church, we are responsible for creating or contributing to the environments we occupy. Our choices determine the course of our culture. If we long for true empowerment, if we aspire to trust others and be trusted, if we crave the productivity and joy of working in environments of grace, how do we bring them about?

For us to make the first move toward an environment of grace, we must realize that we have been influenced by our environments, whether we created them or not. Have you ever experienced an environment of grace? Have you tasted it? Perhaps you felt it around a mentor. Maybe you perceived it at church, or among a special group of friends, or at home, or in a vibrant work setting. Remember what it was like? Remember the impact it had on you? Remember how it lifted you beyond anything you had experienced before?

Real People

The trouble with reading a book that promises so much is the presumption that a book has made you an authority on the subject: "You know they're right. I'm going to teach some people this stuff."

We cannot transfer to others what we are not experiencing ourselves any more than we can come back from where we haven't been.

But to teach these truths and not be engaged in an environment attempting to live out of grace is like trying to teach a skunk to dance: the dancing isn't very impressive, people get scratched, and the whole room stinks.

There is no shortcut, no fix, no Band-Aid. We need to find or return to this kind of environment for the support we need to be an instrument of grace. We cannot transfer to others what we are not experiencing ourselves any more than we can come back from where we haven't been.

Environment represents one rail of the ladder. The other rail is relationships, to which we turn our attention next.

Grabbing Hold

- How does the level of emotional safety in your work environment affect your contribution?
- Do you think the risks of building an environment of grace are worth the rewards?
- In your current work, worship, and home environments, can you identify some of the underlying assumptions that affect those environments?
- What one environment can you begin to have an impact on today?

Chapter Four

Nurturing Relationships That Ground and Sustain Us

We are all angels with only one wing; we can only
fly while embracing one another.

—*Luciano De Crescenzo*

Ruth Peterson was a busy woman in her early forties with a challenging life and an ailing mother. Ruth used to drive three miles to the beach, trying to walk off the pressured cares of life, whenever her world began to close in on her.

One day she met a sweet little six-year-old girl with honey-blonde hair and eyes as blue as the sea, building a sandcastle on the beach. The little girl greeted her. Just then a sandpiper glided by. "That's a joy," said the child.

"It's a what?" asked Mrs. Peterson.

"It's a joy. My mama says sandpipers come to bring us joy."

"Fine," said the depressed Mrs. Peterson. The bird went off down the beach. "Good-bye, joy," she muttered; "Hello, pain."

"What's your name?" the little girl asked.

"I am Ruth Peterson."

"Great! My name's Wendy."

As Ruth left the beach, Wendy called out, "Come again, Mrs. P. We'll have another happy day."

The days and weeks that followed were even more dark-hearted for Ruth, and she found herself walking the beach again. The child she'd forgotten about suddenly appeared.

"Hello, Mrs. P! Do you want to play?"

"Well, let's just walk," Ruth said. "Where do you live?"

"Over there," pointed Wendy. She pointed to a row of summer cottages, which Mrs. Peterson thought strange, since this was midwinter.

"Where do you go to school?" Ruth asked.

"I don't go to school. Mommy says we're on vacation."

When Ruth left for home that day, Wendy said it had been a happy day. Feeling surprisingly better, Ruth smiled at her and had to agree.

Three weeks later, Ruth rushed to the beach in a state of near panic. She was in no mood to greet Wendy when she saw the girl. "If you don't mind," she said sternly, "I'd rather be alone today."

"Why?" asked Wendy.

Ruth turned quickly on her and shouted, "Because my mother died—all right!?" She then caught herself and thought, *Why am I telling this to a little child?*

"Oh," Wendy said quietly. "Then this is a bad day."

"Yes, and yesterday, and the day before, and—oh please, just go away."

"Did it hurt?" Wendy inquired.

"Did *what* hurt?" the exasperated woman replied.

"When she died?"

"Of course it hurt!!!" Ruth snapped. She excused herself and walked swiftly away from the little girl.

A month or so later, Ruth decided to visit the beach again. Wendy wasn't there. Feeling a little guilty and ashamed, she admitted to herself that she had actually missed Wendy. She decided to walk up to the cottage after her walk. She knocked on several doors until one was opened, by a young woman with honey-colored hair.

"Hello, I'm Ruth Peterson. I missed your little girl today."

"Oh yes, Mrs. Peterson, please come in. Wendy spoke of you so much. I'm afraid I allowed her to bother you. If she was a nuisance, please accept my apologies."

"No, not at all. She's a delightful child," Ruth said, suddenly realizing she meant it. "Where is she?"

"Wendy died last week, Mrs. Peterson. She had leukemia. Maybe she didn't tell you." Struck silent, Ruth groped for a chair and caught her breath.

"Wendy left something for you, Mrs. Peterson . . . if only I can find it. Could you wait a moment while I look?"

In a few moments, she handed Ruth a smeared envelope with "MRS P" printed in bold, childlike letters. Inside was a drawing in bright crayon hues—a yellow beach, a blue sea, and a brown bird. Underneath was carefully printed: A *Sandpiper to bring you joy.*

Tears filled Mrs. Peterson's eyes, and a heart that had almost forgotten how to love or trust opened wide. She took Wendy's mom in her arms and muttered, "I'm so sorry. I'm so sorry." And they wept together.

The precious picture of the Sandpiper is framed now and hangs in Mrs. Peterson's study. A gift from a child with sea-blue eyes and hair the color of sand—who gave a hardened, frightened adult the powerful gift of trust, love, and joy.[1]

Hardwired Needs

At various seasons in our lives, we grow numb to the longings of our lives. We get busy. We get distracted and nearly immobilized by the assignments or disappointments of life. We grow unaware of the *needs* in our lives.

God created us with needs. These needs limit us. That's the way God wired us. It is a built-in design feature that allows us to receive love. If love is the process of meeting needs, and in truth it is, then hiding my needs actually hides me from receiving the love of others. Needs require us to be *inter*dependent. When we choose, through pain, fear, or hurt, to live *in*dependently, we act as if we have no needs. What we need most, the love of others, we become tragically insulated from.

A need is anything we require or lack, in order to be fulfilled and productive. It doesn't matter whether we're young or old, childlike, cynical, average or above average, rich or poor, we all have needs . . . all the time. Needs, such as attention, affirmation, acceptance, comfort, correction, intimacy, security, training, support, and a bushel-basket full of others. You can't escape these needs. They're in your custom-designed DNA.

The Sandpiper stories of life take this age-old truth one step further, by underscoring that we have needs that only God and others can meet.[2]

The Radical Catalyst

The most frustrating thing about getting our needs met by others is that it requires *trust*. This is the last thing you want to hear when you have already carefully concluded that no one can be trusted . . . except yourself. "I'll nurture a relationship of trust, all right, just with *myself*. Sorry, I can't go down that trust road anymore. Nice sounding, I'll give you that. But way too much pain, too much risk, too many unmet expectations with the faces of those who failed me brightly etched in my memory. You might have almost convinced me when I was in my teens, but not now. Way too much data standing in the way of believing that pipe dream. Nope. Ain't going there. I may fail, but it will be *me* failing. And I'll have no one to blame but me. I like it that way. I take the blame, I get the credit. I will be the master of my fate, the captain of my soul. Me, I can trust. God, *maybe*. Even he does some weird stuff I can't figure out. But trusting others with me, my dreams, my cherished hopes, you gotta be kidding! I may look like I just fell off the turnip truck, but that's only because I'm bruised from the beating I took trusting others."

Many of us have a prepackaged list of reasons why we're not going to trust others. Mrs. Peterson didn't initially trust Wendy primarily because she couldn't understand what a little girl could possibly contribute to her life. Mrs. Peterson had a plan to work out her desperate situation on her own. She just needed the occasional help of a cool breeze and the white noise of a beach to help her sort out her life.

Some of us no longer trust because we've been badly mistreated by those we thought were trustworthy. We once trusted people who are now known as our *former* friends. Their Christmas cards have been taken out of our photo albums. They caused us pain and disillusionment. It's what prompted Frederick the Great to conclude, "The more I get to know people, the more I love my dog."

Trust is not a native flower in the human heart. Many of us figure we can skip a pile of misery by just trusting ourselves. But this life philosophy ignores the haunting reality that I have *needs* I cannot possibly meet on my own. We know it to be true, in those moments when we lie in our bed, awakened in a cold sweat with the overpowering awareness that we are simply not "making it." The talents, will power, energy, and panache we thought would carry the day have only carried us into despair. In that pure, clean moment of telling myself the truth, I receive the insight that feels as though it came about twenty years too late. I realize that I have pushed away the gifts, resources, and love of others that could keep me from shooting myself in the foot, over and over. It is a painful realization. Because I realize that I cannot access the love and resources of others without *trust*. And my unwillingness to trust is my one protection that I can't give up. It is why so many who have learned not to trust know the surprising ache of being surrounded by people, but feeling all alone.

As Mrs. Peterson eventually rediscovered, trust is the radical catalyst for opening our hearts to grace. For knowing real community. As you will discover, this rail of *relationships of trust* is both the precondition and the result of an environment of grace.

The Tie Between Needs and Trust

It is imperative to understand the relationship between our needs and trust. Reflect on this life-piercing one-liner: *The degree to which*

*The degree to which
I trust you is the
degree to which
you can meet my
needs, no matter
how much love
you have for me.*

I trust you is the degree to which you can meet my needs, no matter how much love you have for me.

You may have great intentions to express grace and love to me. And you may be well aware of my incredible needs that must be met all the time. But here is the painful reality: without trust, no one, not even God, is allowed to meet them!

So, no matter where we are on our journey, our needs cannot be met without relationships of trust. When relationships of this kind work side by side with an environment of grace, they create individuals and cultures in which creativity, hope, integrity, and other positive outcomes emerge.

The significance of the rail of relationships of trust can be demonstrated when we carefully ponder the effect on a life that does not experience the benefits of trust. Without trust:

- I cannot experience love.
- I cannot experience truth.
- I cannot have a relationship with God or with people.
- I cannot be guided into who I am or the fulfillment of my life purpose.
- I cannot develop my competencies, wealth, and power except at the expense of relationships.
- Relationships exist to provide something I want at the expense of what I and others need.
- Character is minimized at the expense of developing competencies.
- Relationships are ineffective, as we lobby for the contribution of our strengths.

- Children live without direction, and the value of life is minimized for the quality of life.
- Truth is relative; I live as my own expert.
- Pleasure is substituted for intimacy.
- Spirituality is performance-based; right behavior is more important than key relationships.
- Power is pursued; the weak are ignored.
- Rights are demanded as the presumed basis for fulfillment.
- I live in isolation; I hide from others, my character is immature, and I am vulnerable to my weaknesses.
- I lose hope.
- I lose my identity.
- My unhealthy self-story feeds my dysfunction.
- I am trapped in a mind-set of "I ought to . . ."
- I can reach my potential but never experience my destiny.

The Outcomes of Untrust

Many still ignore the obvious and try to find fulfillment in isolation. In his classic tale *The Great Divorce*, C. S. Lewis illustrates this point as he recounts a bus ride from hell to heaven. Instead of finding fire in hell, Lewis discovers street after street of rather nice homes, but all had been abandoned. Lewis asked an educated man, "Was there once a much larger population?" His response sent chills down Lewis's spine, even aboard the hot bus:

> Not at all. The trouble is that they're so quarrelsome. As soon as anyone arrives he settles in some street. Before he's been there twenty-four hours he quarrels with his neighbor. Before the week is over he's quarreled so badly that he decides to move. Very likely he finds the next street empty 'cause all the people there have quarreled with their neighbors—and moved. So he settles in. If by any chance the street is full, he goes further. But even if he stays, it makes no

odds. He's sure to have another quarrel pretty soon and then he'll move on again. Finally, he'll move right to the edge of town and build a new house. You see, it's easy here. You've only got to think a house and there it is. That's how the town keeps on growing.[3]

In fear of the potential risks associated with interdependence, we tend to choose isolation over community.

Capacity Ladder Myths

On the capacity ladder, might makes right. We're told that nice people finish last and that the end justifies the means. Notice that the utilitarian nature of the capacity ladder makes the ladder quite portable. As Figure 4.1 illustrates, when relationships get tough, we can fold up the ladder, pack it away, and move it to another location. Only friends, pain, commitments, snapshots, history, love, trust, and dreams stay behind. And we keep getting more and more lonely, more and more guarded, more and more cynical as our families, organizations, and cultures fragment.

There's only one path out of that hellish, swirling eddy. We must finally count the cost of folding the ladder. We must finally come to the realization that we have needs we cannot meet alone. Only then can we stay long enough to learn a process of meeting those needs in community.

When relationships become expendable and expedient, used for gain and then left behind, the relationship rail becomes extremely weak and fragile because such a lifestyle short-circuits the time-intensive process necessary for the meeting of needs. It doesn't happen at a seminar. It doesn't happen in a weekend. It doesn't happen in a memo or at a staff meeting. Rejecting a process of meeting needs, relationships on the capacity ladder turn into a pursuit of personal power over others, evidenced by a constant battle for individual or special rights. Pursuing power over others increases isolation, inhibiting character development. Manipulative, contrived connections may help us acquire certain rights, but they can never meet our deepest needs. These needs can only be met by the gracious care

Figure 4.1. The Portable Capacity Ladder

and concern of others. They cannot be bought, demanded, coerced, manipulated, or extracted through power over others.

Created for Community

Creating community in all our spheres of influence begins when we shift our focus from self to others. We just described the intention of *love*. Meeting the needs of others is an expression of our love. For example, when we listen to a friend, we meet her need for attention. When we affirm a teammate, we meet his need for significance. When we protect those who work under us, we meet their need for security, and so on.

Tim Sanders of Yahoo asks,

What do I mean by "love?" The best general definition that I've read comes from philosopher Milton Mayeroff's brilliant book, *On Caring*. "Love,'" he writes, "is the selfless promotion of the growth of the other." When you help others grow to become the best people that they can be, you are being loving—and as a result, you grow.[4]

A Task Master's Culture

The capacity ladder by itself can lead to task-driven cultures that create people-users—those who use others for their own benefit and to further their own success. Ashleigh Brilliant catches this attitude in the quip from one of his cartoons: "Do your best to satisfy me—that's all I ask of everybody." Conversely, those on the character ladder live for the benefit of others and define success in terms of helping others grow and develop.

Capacity-ladder-only cultures rightly strive for accountability in order to get things done, but they do so at the expense of people's hearts. We see this in families where children are controlled but feel disconnected from the love needed to develop. It shows up in schools where students perform well on tests but don't develop healthy peer relationships. And in businesses where the culture honors the achievement of goals and the earning of profits over the health of its people, leaders and followers quickly learn to hide their hearts in an attempt to reach those goals, even at the expense of their own souls.

Capacity-ladder-only cultures seldom ask the hard questions about how they treat people. As a result, they miss seeing the expanding potential that only relationships of trust can bring out. In the end, if not along the way, it's not how much money we've made or what we've accomplished that brings fulfillment; rather, it is the relationships we have developed that have allowed us to do those things. Fulfillment comes from how well we connect with those around us as we attend school, pursue our careers, raise our families, or volunteer our time. Like a plant with a good root system in the right soil, these connections produce tremendous fruit. What kinds of fruit?

On the character ladder, the depth of influence is honored above the height of position. Living the truth is more important than living for success. Instead of making hasty moves that may harm relational investments, character-ladder leaders protect relationships, even though commitment, patience, and time can be costly. Mistakes and failures are viewed through the farsighted lens of personal development rather than through the nearsighted lens of short-term results. Leaders in relational organizations affirm the wisdom of Winston Churchill when he said, "Success is going from failure to failure with great enthusiasm." Trust develops in such places, and we learn things about each other that we never knew before, finding profound strengths that can be hidden behind roles.

Experiencing Acceptance

One fruit from relationships of trust is the experience of unconditional acceptance. Experiencing and offering acceptance arises from a process requiring frequent, interactive communication in committed relationships of trust. Commitment is very important to environments of acceptance. Acceptance only lasts as long as the commitment lasts because commitment creates a soul connection that takes relationships beyond their utilitarian functions.

To experience acceptance, we must first admit our need for acceptance from others. Then we must take the next step and receive expressions of acceptance from others. Receiving acceptance empowers us to give acceptance. Thousands struggle with accepting others, not realizing that they first have to receive acceptance before they can give it. Did

You and I cannot give acceptance unless we have been willing to receive acceptance.

you get that? *You and I cannot give acceptance unless we have been willing to receive acceptance.* It is not usually just the issue of finding someone to accept us. The real trick is believing in their acceptance.

If people affirm us for who we are, this ignites a healthy desire to please them. If we love and are loved in spite of what we know about others or what they know about us, we become empowered to change for the better. The same proves true in our relationship with God. If we know God loves us, in spite of who we are, this ignites a desire to please him. But if we lack a sense of acceptance, either from God or from others, we become edgy and apprehensive and we second-guess others. So how does one become a person who sows acceptance?

Ron Willingham, whose organization, Integrity Systems, has trained over a million salespeople to be more productive, recognizes our need for acceptance to be and do our best:

> In our courses, we train facilitators to create a non-critical atmosphere and give unconditional acceptance to people. To look at them and see God-valued people. To listen without biases. To listen nonjudgmentally. To look for and focus on their strengths. Many people fight us at first, feeling uncomfortable at receiving unconditional acceptance—not being accustomed to it. Many have suffered abuse, confusion and rejection to the point that unconsciously they aren't comfortable with real acceptance.[5]

To engender an environment of acceptance, there must be an environment of trustworthiness. For the *reception* of acceptance is a trust issue.

Here's another one of those life-piercing one-liners: *I cannot receive your acceptance, no matter how much acceptance you have to give, if I fear trusting you.* When both come together, acceptance and trust, there is a tangible, life-giving freedom released that spreads faster than butter on a warm cinnamon roll.

Looking back on a renowned career that began with his debut at the age of eight with the Budapest Philharmonic, concert pianist Andor Foldes knows the power of discerning encouragement.

> At 16, I was in the midst of a personal crisis arising from differences with my music teacher. Then the renowned pianist Emil von Sauer, Liszt's last surviving pupil, came to Budapest and asked me to play for him. He listened intently to Bach's Toccata in C major and requested more. I put all my heart into playing Beethoven's "Pathetique" sonata and continued with Schumann's "Papillons." Finally, von Sauer rose and kissed me on the forehead. "My son," he said, "when I was your age I became a student of Liszt. He kissed me on the forehead after my first lesson, saying, 'Take good care of this kiss—it comes from Beethoven, who gave it to me after hearing me play.' I have waited for years to pass on this sacred heritage, but now I feel you deserve it."
>
> Nothing in my life has meant as much to me as von Sauer's praise. Beethoven's kiss miraculously lifted me out of my crisis and helped me become the pianist I am today. Soon I in turn will pass it on to the one who most deserves it.
>
> Praise is a potent force, a candle in a dark room. It is magic, and I marvel that it always works.[6]

Telling the Truth

Another fruit of relationships of trust is honesty, which is so rare that Thomas Sowell observed, "There are only two ways of telling the complete truth—anonymously and posthumously." It *is* rare, but it is much less rare and is fully possible in an environment of grace. When we experience grace in spite of our failures, we gain the strength to face the truth without fear. We learn to welcome truth because it no longer threatens the core of our being. For so long, we feared that to receive honest criticism was to admit failure. Such failure would make us unfit, unlovable, unacceptable, unworthy, incapable. We danced around any hint of truth that ran the risk of exposing a weakness or a fault. But when that chip is no longer on the table, when grace tells me that I am loveable, independent of flawless behavior, then I can receive honesty and I can respond in honesty. I then learn an honest assessment of myself, instead of clinging to what life *must* look like to protect my kingdom. Those who live amid ungracious environments learn to hide the truth. They become polished excuse-makers and blame-shifters. This kind of behavior signals imminent danger for any group, company, organization, or family. Further, it destroys any chance of deeper growth for the individual. Character cannot develop without honesty. In contrast, grace nurtures honesty. It releases people to face hard truth, knowing there is a safety net if they fall. We help others, as well as ourselves, when we choose acceptance and truth as the pillars of our relationships.

Our friend John Lynch shares that one of the most difficult and wonderfully important statements of truth ever made to him came, at a board meeting, from one of his closest friends. After John had made, in his opinion, an eloquent and profound statement regarding an issue, his friend said these words:

> John, you are more articulate and eloquent than me. You present your point so forcefully I am tempted to abandon my position on the weight of your overpowering eloquence. But I want you to know, that even though you may win the discussion, and I go quiet, *I am not convinced you are right.*

In an environment of grace, surrounded by relationships of trust, John was undone. He looked around the room hoping to find someone who would say, "No, I don't think that's true. I think John is fair and gentle and accommodating in his reasoning with all of us. I do not know where this attack is coming from, but I think John's gentle sharing of ideas makes St. Frances of Assisi seem harsh and unyielding." But instead, his fellow leaders and dear friends said nothing. It was quiet for a long time before his best friend mumbled, "He's right, you know." It was a meeting that changed John's life.

He could have stood up and, before storming out of the room, yelled, "You don't know me! None of you really know me. This is so unfair!" But he knew too much. He trusted these leaders, and now their honesty would be used to remove blinders from his heart. The community of trusted, honest friends protected John from self-deceptive arrogance and changed the entire environment of their friendships and meetings.

Fruit Within Our Reach

Like acceptance, affirmation, and honesty, relationships of trust can seem like ripe, red, delicious apples hanging just beyond your grasp. You know they would taste great and nourish you, but what good is fruit if you can't get it to your mouth? It's a table decoration, not much more. Years of counterproductive relational and environmental practices may have left you skeptical. But these words about the fruit of gracious community are not intended to tease our hungry soul. The wonderful thing is, relationships of grace can bloom pretty quickly.

For instance, a couple from Mexico came to our training conference in Phoenix. Just a year later, they showed up in Los Angeles, excited to repeat the seminar. When Bruce asked them why, they invited him to have lunch with some friends they had brought along. During the meal, a medical doctor, a school principal, and others shared significant changes that had occurred in their marriages, families, and careers as a result of the influence of that one couple, who, upon returning to Mexico, had shared some of what they had learned about living and working in relationships of trust.

When our needs are met amid relationships of trust, we become fulfilled. In fulfillment, we give back to the community in far greater measure than we could as isolated individuals. When we understand and admit how much we need each other, we can leave behind our overdependence on lonely capacity ladders and begin forming the basis for caring communities where ordinary people can and do accomplish extraordinary things.

Only the character ladder promotes such a sustaining community. It's longer, so it takes more time to climb. It's stronger, so it's able to support more weight at greater heights. It is also more expensive and harder to manufacture.

On the character ladder, relationships of trust (these committed relationships that meet needs) support each rung in tandem with an environment of grace. Every step in the chapters to come will show just how important purposeful, intimate human interactions are in developing, nurturing, and sustaining our character and influence. Relationships provide the context for the affirmation and application of the principles embedded in the rungs.

Fellow Climbers

We believe there is a God-driven movement in this generation of those who have become disillusioned with the capacity-only ladder. It is incomplete. It is lonely. It doesn't satisfy. It doesn't inspire. It doesn't free. It doesn't draw out the best in us. It doesn't sing. It doesn't laugh. It doesn't give life. It doesn't comfort. It doesn't hold up. There is also an emerging generation who are desperately seeking a different kind of ladder. They have observed horrendous world events in recent years and know that love must replace hatred, yet they realize they must journey further to learn how to receive love themselves. They have witnessed the dead dysfunction and hypocrisy in a dozen arenas, and they long to be part of environments that create authenticity. They are ready to receive influence rather than pursue power at the expense of their hearts. They yearn to experience community instead of stand alone, in hidden self-protection. They long to create environments that inspire the soul.

If you're ready for the journey, let's embark on a climb that will take you above and beyond your best to find God's best. Having learned about the rails of environment and relationships, we are ready to test the rungs.

Grabbing Hold

- Which ladder best describes the environment and relationships of your life right now?

- Because fulfillment requires that we receive acceptance, affirmation, and other expressions of love, why do some people work exclusively for wealth, position, and status?

- What needs do you think you have?

Chapter Five

The First Rung

Stepping Up Through an Act of Trust

> It is a dangerous business to arrive in eternity with
> possibilities which one himself has prevented from
> becoming actualities. Possibility is a hint from God.
> A person must follow it . . . if God does not want
> it, then let him hinder it; the person must not
> hinder it himself.
>
> —*Søren Kierkegaard*

Five years into their marriage, Bill's wife, Grace, chose a creative way to get his attention. One evening when he got home from work, she greeted him at the door with a blunt directive: "We need to go for a ride."

Her strained tone and piercing eyes told Bill she had something important on her mind. Very astutely he reasoned, "I'm in big trouble," and tried to stall by asking, "What about the kids?"

"I took care of them," Grace replied. "They'll be fine."

Heading to their old Chrysler, Bill worried, "What did I do? What did she find out?" By the time he had settled behind the wheel, he had compiled his initial list of defenses and alibis. "Where to?" he asked with feigned, cucumber-coolness.

"Drive north," she said.

They drove for the longest thirty minutes of Bill's life. He didn't say a word and neither did Grace, until she instructed him to pull into an almost empty parking lot. Although his sweat had now soaked through his suit, he wasn't about to let her see his nervousness, so he kept quiet. Grace had never done anything even remotely like this before. This was her call.

Bill could see she had prepared well for this moment. Her peace and clear presence of mind further unnerved him. After a long pause, Grace finally spoke.

"I want you to know that you are a great father, a good provider, and I know that you love me, but I am extremely unhappy, and . . ."

"What? How dare you!" Bill interrupted.

"Yes, I am a good father." He told himself, "I work hard for my family. How can she say she's not happy? This isn't about me. It's about her. She's got a problem."

Continuing to vent his angry response, Bill blurted out other personal accolades. But they didn't work. So he got out of the car and stormed around, playing the wounded spouse role to the hilt. When he finally got back into the car, Grace was still calm and peaceful, completely unmoved by his antics. Then, very simply, she asked, "Don't you want to know why I am so unhappy?"

"Well . . . uh . . . yes," Bill responded. "Why?"

"You will not let me love you," she replied. Then, after a brief pause, "You do not even try to trust me. I love you. I want to be all I can for you, but you won't let me. Please hear me."

Tears filled her eyes. "This is so serious," Grace continued. "You cannot just love me. To have a relationship, I have to be able to love you!" She explained how Bill's inability to trust was slowly decaying their marriage and his relationship with his kids.

For five years Bill had kept his life hidden from Grace. He tested her love in many ways, not willing to believe it could be trusted. He felt she would not be able to handle the real Bill. Each rejection of her sincere, loving attempts to win his heart had caused Grace tremendous pain. Yet, in the face of it all, instead of using condemnation or put-downs, she responded with strength and deep commitment, giving Bill the courage to open his life for review by someone who loved him deeply. According to Bill, "For the first time, I chose to trust Grace with me."

Beginning the Climb

Here's where we begin our climb up the character ladder: *with an act of trust*. This act of trust is distinguished from the relationships of trust we've been discussing that form one of the rails of the ladder. This act of trust actually forms the basis of the first rung. It's here where many of us will try to excuse ourselves from the ladder, even before we get on. "Well, see, this can't be for me, because I'm not able to trust anyone around here."

So what do I do if that's my story? This act of trust is not fully dependent upon the trustworthiness of the environment in which I find myself. It sure helps, but it's not imperative. Sometimes we stumble into cultures of trust, and sometimes we must initiate the first step in faith because the environment does not promote trust. It's possible to be in relationships of trust and *not* trust. And it's possible to be in relationships of untrust and *initiate* trust. If I find myself in such an untrusting and untrustworthy environment, I can be used to change the culture and climate by initiating beginning attempts at trust. I can then become the very conduit to promote a radical environmental change.

We all entrust ourselves to a certain extent to something, whether it's God, money, friends, our spouse, our career, our productivity, ourselves. Such trust—often referred to as faith—lives at the center of our lives, shaping who we are. The impetus to take a step of faith begins in the heart—the inner part of us that longs to be known but is never fully knowable by anyone but our Creator.

With each interpersonal interaction, a struggle of trust ensues. We groan inwardly, longing for a soul mate who truly understands us: "Do you see my potential? Can you see the real me struggling to get out? Can I trust you to see and accept what emerges?"

And yet deep inside, the thought of being completely known terrifies us. We ask ourselves, What would people think if they knew the naked truth about me? Would their friendship and love endure if they knew how I sometimes act and feel?

Bill had asked himself these questions a thousand times. Now they all boiled down to a single question: Could trusting my wife with who I am help fix my heart?

Choices of the Heart

The heart—the inner life, shaped primarily by trust—molds our motives. Our motives establish our values. And our values govern our actions. What we believe about ourselves takes root and is nourished in our hearts. And it's from the heart that our destiny— our ultimate influence and value—flows.

No matter how secret we think they are, we expose our heart beliefs through the choices we make. If we have faith in a bridge, we will trust it enough to drive over it. If we have faith in our spouse, we will choose to reveal ourselves to him or her. If we trust in God, our faith will enable us to escape being molded by circumstances or seduced by compromising opportunities as we move toward making the best life-choices.

Risky Business

Trust is often spelled R-I-S-K. The possibility of betrayal makes trust a risky business. And the risks aren't limited to the sphere of human interaction. Like the friends of the biblical figure Job, many of us question God, particularly when unreasonably bad things happen to reasonably good people. The risk in trust presents a significant quandary in our climb up the character ladder because the first rung is all about trust. First we must trust God and, in turn, trust others (see Figure 5.1). But what motivates us to take this initial step?

For most of us, it comes in the form of a life crisis. There must be sufficient pain to take the first step. I must see that what I am doing isn't working before the myth of self-sufficiency can be debunked. For most of us, it takes a rock mercifully thrown through our plate-glass lives to shatter that myth: the confrontation by a spouse, the time of facing our own mortality or that of a loved one,

Figure 5.1. The First Rung of the Character Ladder

the loss of a special relationship, the unraveling of a life-long dream. In a sense, we must let our seed of destiny fall to the ground and be buried, because this is the only way it can begin to germinate and grow.[1]

We must awaken to our need for God and others. Whatever hinders our character, whatever prevents us from reaching our destiny—these things awaken us to our needs. Needs like these can be met only by placing trust in God and others. It is our need for God's care and commitment and for others' care and commitment that motivates us to take the first step in climbing the character ladder. Without an awareness of our needs, the step is impossible to take.

The Nature of God

When we reflect on the nature of our Creator, we gain a sense of these deeper needs of our heart. The degree to which we entrust ourselves to God demonstrates the level at which we have understood his character. Each of us must ask: Is God good or capricious? Is my Creator personal and intimately aware of my life or just some impersonal force that set things spinning in motion? Is he committed to protecting me or prone to abandoning me when troubles come? Is he a kindly, forgetful, grandfatherly type of deity, who can't quite remember what day it is or who did what? (Was that Mussolini who caused all that trouble in Europe, or was it Ricky Ricardo? Danged if I can remember.) Only if we trust that God is good by nature, we will honor God's authority and power in our lives.

Too many of us have developed a twisted picture of an angry God on too much coffee. Humorist Dave Barry reflects that concept:

> All my religious training was in Sunday school maybe 25 years ago,
> and the main thing I remember was that God was always smiting the
> Pharisees. At least I think it was the Pharisees. It seemed that hardly
> a day went by when they didn't get the tar smitten out of them,
> which is probably why you see so few of them around anymore.[2]

Maybe it's easiest to explain the impact of understanding God's nature and authority by comparing the first steps of the capacity and character ladders. At the bottom of the capacity ladder, we focus on discovering what "I can do," whereas on the character ladder we focus on discovering what God can do. Early on the capacity ladder, we awaken to our potential *for* God—what we think we can offer to God and this world. On the character ladder, we awaken to our destiny *under* God.

On the first step of the capacity ladder, I begin to let me be me, seeking my own unique way in the world. But on the first step of the character ladder, I choose to let God be God, understanding that his ways are not mine. Of course, after we've spent a lot of time on the character ladder our ways come to more closely resemble God's ways. Everything I *do* begins to reflect who God is and who he has created me to *be*. This blending of our desires and God's intentions for us is the goal of the character ladder.

Humble Beginnings

The first rung leads us to humility. Some people assume that learning about the Creator's bigness will lead to a negative assessment of our own smallness as creatures. It can feel almost holy, humble, and pious to demean ourselves:

> Oh, Lord, I am vermin, fit for extinction. That Thou would look upon me without turning me into so much broth is beyond my squirrel-like brain. I am nothing. No, I am less than nothing. Less than the thought of nothing. Less than no thought of nothing, remembered by no one. I am like the bleached cartilage of a thousand generations of parasitic leeches, washed up upon the forgotten shore of demise. This I am and have become. And for this I deserve to be forgotten, dismissed, dispelled and displaced. That Thou doth expend one third of a moment to consider my loathsome frame, is beneath Your greatness, as a slug is beneath yet unnamed galaxies whose citizens can fashion a shovel simply by thinking it to be so. Amen.

Thoughts of false self-deprecation do not honor the nature and authority of God; they demean it. After all, he called creation good, including humans. Such negative self-statements only reveal a poor self-image or a false spirituality, not true humility. Ken Blanchard says,

> People with humility don't think less of themselves, they just think of themselves less. It's healthy to feel good about yourself. . . . The problem is with the ego. Someone once told me that *ego* stands for "Edging God Out." When we get a distorted image of our own importance and see ourselves as the center of the universe, we lose touch

with who we really are as children of God. Our thinking blurs. We lose the sense of our connection with others and with our true selves.

Blanchard also believes that

there are two types of ego-centeredness: *self-doubt* and *false pride*. Both are enemies of humility. People with self-doubt are consumed with their shortcomings and tend to be hard on themselves. People with false pride think they don't need grace and are out of touch with their own vulnerability to sinfulness. Both have a hard time believing that they are loved.[3]

God has no desire for us to belittle ourselves. When we come face-to-face with the strength of God—not as worthless people but as people who are willing to present all our strengths, talents, and influence to the strong hands of a loving Creator—we demonstrate our trust in his nature and authority. Entrusting ourselves to God is the result of a proper understanding of humility. "Humble yourselves, therefore, under God's mighty hand, that he may lift you up in due time."[4] You've just seen a snapshot of the character ladder. People who let God be God and entrust their lives to him understand he has the ultimate responsibility for determining their value and destiny.

> *Unless we trust God with our potential, we will be robbed of his plan for our destiny.*

Leaving our value and destiny in God's hands can be disconcerting for those who have not come to terms with the reality of a loving, personal God. Don't miss this: *Unless we trust God with our potential, we will be robbed of his plan for our destiny.*

This is why humility is so important. It comes back to those vertical rails. God's plan for our destiny involves meaningful interaction with others in communities and environments of grace. We must interact with others who, like us, need grace: people who have their own agendas, weaknesses, sins, and flawed motives; people with strengths, love, and inspiring vision; people who come into our lives with a mixed bag of strengths and weaknesses—traits that engender trust and attributes that give us good reason to write them off. Yet they are all part of God's plan for preparing us for our legacy. God created us for community. God created us to trust and love him and to trust and love others with the deepest parts of our lives. That trust is only possible with humility.

Choosing to love and trust people, especially those who are different from ourselves, has a lot to do with trusting the One who is managing the path of our lives. When we understand and trust that our destiny rests in God's hands, we can endure negative circumstances and difficult relationships with greater patience. More important, as was the case with Bill and Grace, we gain the strength we need to trust people who have our best interests at heart, even at the risk of pain or personal loss. Why? Because we believe that God will somehow work it out for our good, no matter what happens.[5]

Genuine Humility

When we entrust ourselves to God in this way, humility creates increasing gratitude and decreasing greed. Those who learn to trust God have less and less desire to possess somebody else's stuff in order to be content. Whenever we encounter greed, lust, or avarice in a person, we can be sure there is a lack of trust in God at the root. Lack of trust also produces lack of gratitude. Perhaps this is why God began the Ten Commandments with "I am the Lord your God . . . you shall have no other gods before me," and concluded with, "You shall not covet . . . anything that belongs to your neighbor."[6] Entrusting ourselves to God—genuine humility—leads to a thankful, contented heart. One is a prerequisite for the other.

Of course, finding such genuine humility in anyone even most of the time is a tall order. We have all been hurt before by imperfect people and can identify with the cartoon character who complains to his companion: "We've been through so much together . . . and most of it was your fault." Choosing whom to trust can be a messy business. We can't trust just anyone with our innermost being, even if he or she asks us to. This would be foolish and might do more harm than good. But we've got to trust *someone,* so it becomes a question of whom. The answer is closer at hand than you may think. Trust begins with relationships between ordinary people. It starts with those God has placed in our lives.

The second-century theologian Irenaeus said, "The glory of God is a person fully alive." Do you want to experience moments of what it is to be fully alive? Do you desire to leave a legacy for the benefit of future generations? Do you long to experience a greater purpose in life that will sustain you in hard circumstances? Do you crave relationships of trust where you are fully known and know others more fully? Do you hunger for the day when what you do flows completely out of who you are? If so, take the first step up the character ladder.

> *The glory of God is a person fully alive.*
>
> —Irenaeus

With eyes wide open, take a step of faith and make the intentional choice to begin trusting God and others with you. Trust the protection of the Almighty to guard you. He is big enough to keep you safe as you entrust yourself to those who can be trusted. Step up. Then prepare for the next rung.

Grabbing Hold

- Who trusts you?
- How do your actions substantiate the value you place on humility?
- What does hiding what is true about you cost you? What does it cost others?

Chapter Six

The Second Rung

Choosing Vulnerability

One of the reasons our society has become such a
mess is that we're isolated from each other.
—*Maggie Kuhn*

Eight-year-old Bruce and his neighborhood gang were practicing
"evasive maneuvers" one day, not far from his home. They were
"bivouacking" through a dense forest when Bruce drifted off course
and got hopelessly lost. First, he remembers trying to be brave like
"a real soldier." Then the fear of being *really* alone enveloped him.
Lost in a dark jungle, separated from his group, his imagination
took over. This was going to be a short life! In an instant, panic and
terror gripped his heart.

In adult life, many of us wander into dark forests of isolation *on
purpose*. We don't live alone; we just live apart from the benefit of
significant others speaking into our lives. We feel more comfortable
with isolation than with letting others get close. We depend on distance for protection. Although most of us want deeper intimacy, we
fear the pain that such exposure might involve more than we fear
the loneliness of our soul. At least we tell ourselves so.

The Dark Wood

Lonely people are everywhere, anesthetized by popularity, success,
power, or wealth. Many will wake up one day to find themselves
like the character in Dante's *Divine Comedy*: "In the middle of the
road of my life I awoke in a dark wood where the true way was

wholly lost." Although they are surrounded by people, they can't seem to connect in meaningful ways. Suffering from their self-imposed separation, they lose the opportunity to positively influence others. They also lose the opportunity to develop character.

A number of years ago, in graduate school, Bruce created a project around a particular dysfunction he noticed in leaders: deception. He titled it, "Everybody Lies, But Leaders Do It Better." He interviewed leaders from the fields of medicine, journalism, law and law enforcement, the church, and other vocations who had been publicly caught in deception.

The interviews exposed *isolation* as the primary reason the leaders give themselves permission to lie—not a physical but a soul separation from others. Often, the further up leaders are on the capacity ladder or the longer they've occupied its top rung, the worse the problem gets.

Isolation robs a person, leader or not, of the opportunity to grow in the critical areas of self-understanding, self-acceptance, and character. Such a person is caught in the tension between wanting to be known, loved, and accepted and the fear that if others saw through the window of their lives, they would turn away in disgust.

Howard Hendricks, the founder of a respected leadership center in Dallas, said on this subject, "When I meet with leaders, I simply assume society has infected them and they have not lived in authentic communities and that this reality will eventually hurt them."[1]

Getting Out of the Woods

How do we overcome the isolation that threatens to rob us of character growth and influence? The answer is found on the second rung on the character ladder: *choose vulnerability* (see Figure 6.1).

What *is* vulnerability? To be vulnerable means to choose to come under another's influence. It is a choice of the heart to admit that I am in need of another's loving direction and input.

Some time ago, a widely respected business leader taught Bruce several helpful skills in dealing with people. However, as Bruce grew

Figure 6.1. The Second Rung of the Character Ladder

to know this man, he began to resist the leader's influence. It wasn't an intentional resistance, just an instinctive hesitation.

Intuitively, Bruce understood that by giving this man authority, he would be giving him influence since authority involves influence, which, in turn, helps shape destiny. However, this man was not the kind of leader who would submit to the counsel of others. He shared much about his life but was not knowable or teachable in critical areas. Automatically, Bruce biased himself against this man's teaching and mentoring because he concluded that, despite his amazing gifts and abilities, he could not be completely trusted.

We have all had experiences like this, where holes in the character of others have caused us to pull back from their influence.

However, we must not let this become an excuse to avoid the positive influence of others. It must not keep us from our need to be vulnerable.

Example of a Vulnerable Leader

The famous politician William Wilberforce once faced this issue of vulnerability. As a personal friend of William Pitt, the soon-to-be prime minister of Great Britain, Wilberforce's early political career looked rather bright, even though his personal life and character seemed a bit wanting. As a popular member of Parliament, Wilberforce relished his power and prestige and especially the parties around London, which he frequented with gusto. But through the encouragement of an old college friend, Isaac Milner, a tutor at Queen's College Cambridge, Wilberforce began to take a serious look at his life, leading to an encounter with the claims of Jesus. After much personal struggle, Wilberforce trusted God with his destiny and began his ascent up the character ladder. He considered the implications of his decision to trust God, soon concluding through personal study that he should leave politics and become a minister. Thankfully, Wilberforce's personal study also convinced him that he should go to his trusted friends and ask their counsel.

First he went to Pitt. Pitt wanted Wilberforce as a political ally, especially with his recently improving reputation. So he asked Wilberforce to stay in politics. But the advice of one person, even a significant person, wasn't enough to convince Wilberforce. Wrestling with his conscience, he sought out John Newton, the author of the hymn "Amazing Grace." Surely Newton would understand his desire to pursue the ministry. Instead, the former slave trader agreed with Pitt and encouraged Wilberforce to hang on to his political position and to use his know-how to champion worthy causes.

No one knows just how much Wilberforce struggled to open his life to the commentary and counsel of others. But it could not have been easy. How do we know? How many people have you approached and shared the desires of your heart, asking not for their advice but counsel to sort it out? How did it feel listening to their answers? Have you had to go as far as Wilberforce, following the advice of others, even when it feels like it would work against his (or your) own best interests?

Conquering the Fears Within

Choosing vulnerability is tough work. As we open the shades and let others look inside, we may not like what people say they see. They may see the "stuff" we thought was well hidden under the bed, weaknesses we'd rather not admit. But they may also discover valuable treasures we assumed were just old yard-sale junk. The crisis comes when they recognize our true talents and character and challenge us to move beyond our excuses and exercise our strengths. That's when it feels like wise friends have suddenly become dullards, meddling in places where they shouldn't.

Bill once mentored a man who faced this crisis. Austin excelled in sports throughout his college years, and he also excelled academically, bringing some great job options at graduation. After launching into his career, Austin rose quickly through the ranks. But when the chief executive invited him to join the top brass, Austin turned him down. A bit later, he decided to leave the company altogether, even though those closest to him believed he was perfectly suited for what he had been doing.

When Bill quizzed him about this, Austin brushed it aside, at least for a while. Later Austin confided, "How could I have given up such an opportunity?" The more they talked, over time, the clearer it became that Austin didn't feel worthy of being among the top brass or in *any* leadership position. Thinking together through his life, they began to notice a pattern. The closer Austin grew to positions of authority and influence, the more nervous and fearful he became. Bill asked him if he thought he could have handled the positions he had turned down. He responded immediately, "Yes, without a doubt." But his fear of recognition and honor caused him to "humbly" decline advancement opportunities.

Caught in a false view of humility rooted deep in his personal belief system and upbringing, Austin made choices contrary to his abilities and potential and then had to live with the pain of lost opportunities. Although he looked extremely competent on the outside, Austin struggled with deep fears on the inside.

Malachy McCourt, a twentieth-century Horatio Alger, came to New York from the slums in Ireland in 1952 and made a name for himself as an actor and man-about-town. But his outward success didn't protect him from the malicious inner voice that haunts many of us.

> I was fit; healthy, and young with a vast panorama of life and lust ahead. Still, there were days when I was stuck with my own company, and all the interior demons seized the opportunity to remind me I was a loser, an idiot; lacking in decency and intelligence; and one day "they," the ubiquitous "they," would find out that I was from the slums of Limerick, that I'd failed everything except reading and writing in our school, Leamy's National School, known to us as the Leamy College of Surgeons because the masters cut us up so much. In reality, the school was operating as a holding pen for potential convicts. . . . So it was for me at Leamy's. I learned about fear; terror; and foreboding. I learned what a useless lump of lard I was and how I would never amount to anything.[2]

Most of us struggle with self-doubts and the fear of being found out. It is always out there, or better, in here, like a Judas seeking to betray us into the hands of our accusers. Fear of rejection, fear of failure, fear of success, fear of commitment, fear of abandonment—all skew our choices in panicked directions. Often the insight and counsel of others is the only light that will expose these fears and encourage us to move toward our God-ordained destiny. Vulnerability helps move us beyond the limits imposed by our fears.

Beyond Transparency

Vulnerability also moves us beyond transparency. Transparency is a good start, but it doesn't go far enough. Transparency is simply disclosing yourself to others at times but in ways that you control. Many people reveal multiple areas of difficulty in their lives (such as problems with impatience or anger) only when they can maintain control of what they do with their admission. Or they are willing to address the issues, but only privately, without letting anyone have access to them in those areas. The more eloquent we are, the more skillfully we may remain *selectively transparent*—a clever means of remaining isolated.

In vulnerability, you deliberately place yourself under the influence of others, submitting yourself to their strengths. You give them the right to know the pain of your weaknesses and to care for you. You choose to let others know you, to have access to your life, to teach you, and to influence you.

In part, this true vulnerability is what the Bible means when it speaks of submission. *Submission* is a love word, not a control word to be slapped on others like a choke collar. Submission means letting someone love us, teach us, or influence us. In fact, the degree to which we submit to others is the degree to which we will experience their love, regardless of how much they love us. Submission goes hand in hand with vulnerability.

When Bruce was in his late twenties, an esteemed board of a growing organization invited him to join their team. However, five friends objected and blocked that appointment. As members of the organization, they did not trust his leadership to the point of letting him become a director. This rejection became one of life's most painful circumstances, as Bruce thought, "My friends have turned on me." Yet the event became a "turning point" lesson in vulnerability. He chose to go to each of these friends and hear their counsel on what they perceived to be his weaknesses, even though he knew this action would not reverse the hurtful decision.

Defining Integrity

Let's look at the progression. Vulnerability causes people to know your life is open to them. You are teachable. You will allow the cracks in your character to be not only seen but filled, as you receive their influence. This process expresses your integrity to others and reinforces it to yourself.

In one sense, integrity is an uncompromising adherence to truth. The Hebrew concept of integrity includes straightness, as opposed to crookedness. This meaning has carried forward to our day. Crooked people lack integrity. Stealing from an employer makes you a crook.

But integrity has to go deeper than the skin. Many pursue an uncompromising adherence to truth for its own sake, as if this brand of integrity makes them better than everyone else. We've all met people like this. They wear their integrity like a medal pinned to their swelled chests.

Pursuing integrity solely as a virtue is futile, even destructive to authentic integrity, especially when such pretenders try to point out the character flaws of others by the glint off their self-awarded medals.

Pursuing integrity is not just for our benefit. It doesn't earn us any extra credit. Instead, integrity must be pursued as a heart quality that enables us to be love-givers and truth-tellers among those we influence. Our integrity is always for the benefit of those we influence.

Our integrity is always for the benefit of those we influence.

What a difference it would make if we understood that the pursuit of virtue is not to become someone others call virtuous. Pursuing virtue is for the purpose of gaining permission so we can influence those we love. Isn't that the coolest thought?

We soon learn that vulnerability triggers two relational effects. First, people gain access to your life as you submit to their influence. Second, you are given access to their lives, as they trust you and see that you are open to them. This kind of relationship is called authentic.

Expanding Influence

In taking this second step up the character ladder, we must remember, first, that vulnerability means coming under another's influence and submitting to the love they offer, and second, that vulnerability both expresses and sustains integrity, which enables others to trust us enough to submit to our influence. Earning others' trust leads to a natural third result: expanded influence. How does that happen?

> *Vulnerability both expresses and sustains integrity, which enables others to trust us enough to submit to our influence.*

Consider how Bruce's potential mentor, to whom we alluded earlier in this chapter, lost the substantial influence he could have had with Bruce. Because of this person's isolation, Bruce simply could not trust him, and his influence declined.

Recall Bruce's five friends—the ones who rejected his board nomination. Bruce and these friends have influenced many others and accomplished many projects together that would have been relinquished if Bruce had remained in isolation. Now multiply that near-loss by thousands of organizations and healthy relationships and significant world-changing activities that have been forfeited, and you have some idea of the importance of vulnerability in reaching our destiny.

What do you need to do in order to grow in this area? How about finding at least one trusted friend to meet with regularly and give him or her permission to take a fresh look at your choices: someone with whom you can pull back the shades a bit and let your heart be revealed; someone who can help you face your fears; some-one you trust to give you a "second opinion" on what you may be going through. As Julia Gatta has pointed out, "Experience, no matter how accurately understood, can never furnish its own inter-pretation." Depth perception is impossible with only one eye.

Vulnerability leads into seemingly dangerous places. Vulnera-bility conjures up synonyms like *unguarded, unsafe, defenseless, naked,* and *susceptible.* Little wonder so many would rather skip it. Why should we open ourselves to the possibility of more pain? Because "growth," as Gail Sheehy notes, "demands a temporary surrender of security." Here's the only possible reason: God accom-plishes some of his best work in dangerous places, including deep-ening our integrity and enlarging our spheres of influence. We soon discover that vulnerability is a beautiful gift, given not only to releasing our strengths for the benefit of others. It's also the "encryption key" to finding out who we really are.

John came on staff into a church environment where vulnera-bility was valued as much as his talents and competency:

I was undone. Here I was with all my scholarly books, my winsome-ness, my eloquence and snappy humor. These were supposed to carry the day. These would be my calling card that would allow me to stay needed, that would propel me into my significance. These would grant me authority and position and retirement benefits. And sud-denly I felt trapped in an environment that paid no particular homage to my greatness. I began to realize that the basis of whether I made it here had little to do with being able to keep banging out compelling messages. They had already chosen to love me and let me grow up past my vaunted view of myself and my messages. The basis of whether I would "make it" here would be my vulnerability. Would I let others love me? Would I let them into my life? Would I allow myself to gradually take off the competency mask and reveal myself? Would I learn to trust those I'd minister shoulder to shoul-der with? I must tell you, the whole environment scared me nearly to death. I resented it at first. I almost ran someplace else where I'd be revered for my talents. But the damage had been done. I was falling in love with being known. I was learning a whole new way of life. I had come to this group of bumpkins convinced that I could move them slowly along to some semblance of maturity, only to find that they were tolerating my arrogance because they saw the real John underneath. They patiently waited for the environment of love and grace to do its work. And now, eighteen years later, like the Velveteen Rabbit, I am becoming real amongst other rabbits who are becoming real. Go figure.

Breaking the Pattern of Invulnerability

Invulnerability, along with the unhealthy isolation engendered by lack of trust, creates an environment in which character development is always at risk. Breaking the pattern with grace always starts small, with everyday choices.

Ken remembers going to a staff meeting after a conference a while back. Inevitably, the question is asked, "How are you?" Often, it is just an agreed-upon way of saying, "Hey, we're here and by golly, isn't that good and everything?" Except this time, Ken's teammates prodded for a truthful response rather than the typical small-talk answer. Ken balked. He didn't want them to know how tired and weak and weary he was, although all this showed clearly in his work, attitude, and physical demeanor. Ken wanted to appear strong. But they asked again, "How are you, really?"

He hesitated, not sure what they would say if he admitted his weakness. But he knew he trusted them. So, he figured, "What have I got to lose?" He told them how deeply exhausted he was, so tired he couldn't think straight. He tried to explain how he felt without being embarrassed, but he couldn't. Being vulnerable in a "corporate" setting was so unfamiliar to him.

This is how his team responded. One staff member said, "We believe you. How can we help?"

Another said, "I know how we can help. You need to take some time off. When's the last time you and your wife just took off alone together?"

Still another offered, "Will you let me plan the trip for you?" They identified Ken's need to be believed. They identified his need to have the details taken care of. (Ken is lousy at planning time off.) They responded with acceptance and affirmation and with tangible offers of assistance.

In such an environment, you'd think allowing yourself to be vulnerable would be easy, but we assure you it is not. Doing so is always a choice. And sometimes the advice and counsel of others can be hard to hear. But the payback is huge, especially when we follow our vulnerability with the next step.

Moving Up

The first rung is trusting God and others with me. The second is choosing vulnerability. The second depends on the first. We can find ourselves on more than one rung at a time; such is the nature of truth interplaying with the heart. But usually the third rung depends on the second: we pursue intentional vulnerability so we can go above and beyond our personal best.

Are you tired of living in the "dark wood," feeling isolated and lost though surrounded by others? Do you know two or more people you trust implicitly? Are you willing to come under their influence in a much deeper way than you ever considered before? Are you ready to be vulnerable enough to earn their trust? Becoming vulnerable will both enhance your integrity and express it to others. Does this appeal to you? If so, call those people. Schedule a time to get together and tell them what's in your heart. Choose vulnerability. As with each of us who have contributed to this book, it will take you into a world you may not have known existed.

Grabbing Hold

- What causes you to fear vulnerability?
- Are you willing to trust others with your vulnerability to avoid isolation?
- How much of what you do is truly a reflection of who you are? Why?
- How do you protect and care for those who have been vulnerable with you?

Chapter Seven

The Third Rung

Aligning with Truth

Whenever two people meet there are really six people present. There is each man as he sees himself, each as the other person sees him, and each man as he really is.

—William James

At the early age of twenty-four, a floundering Vincent van Gogh received a letter from his elder brother Theo strongly encouraging him to become an artist. Although others had already begun to treat Vincent's passionate leanings with skepticism, Theo understood him best and remained his closest confidant and ally. Still, Vincent refused his brother's advice. Instead, he left a promising career as an art dealer and began studying to become a teacher. A harmful pattern had begun.

Within the year, it became apparent to all that Vincent would not make it through the rigorous training required of teachers. He had neither the temperament nor the talent for it. Again he asked Theo for advice. But against the urgings of Theo, his parents, and other near relatives, Vincent decided to become an evangelist. The harmful pattern continued.

What pattern? If his sister-in-law's analysis is true—and from Vincent's own letters it appears to be—van Gogh had a difficult time receiving the counsel and concern of others. Vincent had a warped view of humility. Instead of trusting God and others with himself, he trusted only himself with himself. He consistently refused counsel, particularly the counsel of those who loved and cared about him. Artists are *supposed* to be eccentric, but this was just pride and arrogance.

Some people try to emulate Vincent, believing they can maintain a Lone Ranger–type, or vertical, relationship with God while avoiding the horizontal relationships of human interaction. They believe they can experience all that God has for them without receiving the love of others. They may even see this self-sufficiency as a sort of super spirituality. But it doesn't work. Ever. In fact, the life of Jesus is its greatest refutation. This messiah was no monk. He chose to live, laugh, work with, and make himself vulnerable to twelve very fallible and very ordinary men. He allowed several women, such as Mary and Martha of Bethany and even a prostitute, Mary Magdalene, to minister to his needs. He chose vulnerability over a lifestyle of isolation. Van Gogh recoiled from such vulnerability. As his romantic ideals of personal isolation and rugged individualism held sway, Vincent chose to abandon virtually all his relationships, save the one with Theo (by a fragile thread), almost starving himself to death in the impoverished coal town of Borinage. Refusing to heed Theo's urgings to trust his artistic gift and rejecting the counsel of the church leaders about his service, van Gogh wallowed in self-pity over his failures. His remorse brought him to the point of abandoning his faith.

He grew thoroughly disappointed in a God who had not rewarded his self-denial and seemingly pure aspirations to love his fellow humans. Oddly enough, he never considered that God, rather than abandoning him, had perhaps been speaking to him all along through those who loved him.

The Lost Art of Listening

Seeking the counsel of those who know and love us is a good practice on both ladders. On the capacity ladder, when we reach the point at which we become aware of our strengths and talents, it is a good thing to ask and let others ask hard questions: Do I show promise as an artist? Can I do the math it takes to be an engineer?

When we refuse such vulnerability, we can miss our calling altogether, unless we stumble upon it much later in life, as Vincent did.

In a particularly dark moment, he wrote to Theo, "I said to myself, I'll take up my pencil again, I will take up drawing, and from that moment everything has changed for me."[1]

He had finally found his calling. But in doing so, he abandoned the relationships he longed for and needed in order to climb the character ladder, including his relationship with the Caller. As a result, his capacities for creating art became a curse to him instead of a blessing. Throughout his artistic career, Vincent persisted in ignoring the advice of those who cared deeply for him, leaving a trail of broken relationships in his wake. He pursued his painting with a commitment bordering on madness. Obsessed with his ideas, he demanded that people accept his terms for living and loving. His lonely life became representative of the romantic notion of the "starving artist"—a person misunderstood and unloved by an antagonistic culture.

Starving for Love

Van Gogh certainly made his mark on the world of art, but he never reached his goal of living selflessly for others. According to Vincent's sister-in-law,

> It was his aim to humble himself, to forget himself, to sacrifice every personal desire—that was the ideal he tried to reach as long as he sought his refuge in religion, and he never did a thing by halves. But to follow the paths trodden by others, to submit to the will of other people, that was not in his character, he wanted to work out his own salvation.[2]

A bitter and lonely person, Vincent ended his own life with a bullet. He could not work out his own salvation. He could not love others because he was not fulfilled himself. He would not allow God or others to meet his deepest needs. This was the greatest tragedy.

Imagine what van Gogh could have produced had he found his ideal of a *plein air* community of artists pursuing art for the common person. Unfortunately, his attempts stumbled over his desire to control and manipulate others. He drove people away from him, the artist Paul Gauguin being the most memorable example. He would not allow them to address his personality flaws, weaknesses, or poor habits. His art didn't bring him down; his heart did.

Aligning with Truth

The character ladder is not as concerned with "what we do" as it is with "who we are." Its emphasis is on human "being" more than human "doing." Instead of the "What" questions, it asks the "Why" questions: Why do I want this job? Why do I want to pursue this relationship? Why do I think my life would be better if I . . . ?

When we ascend the first and second rungs of the character ladder, entrusting our needs to God and others and choosing to open our lives for their review and input, we soon face the next step: *align with truth*. Thomas Aquinas and the Scholastics defined truth as "the equivalence of the thought with the thing." When we say something is true we mean it conforms to reality, to what is. The questions we must ask on this rung are meant to bring our perception of ourselves into line with what those who know us affirm as real. Do I believe it is true? Will I listen to what they say? Will I follow their advice? (See Figure 7.1.)

This is the true test of character: not just coming under others' influence but acting on the wisdom and truth of their counsel.

This is the true test of character: not just coming under others' influence but acting on the wisdom and truth of their counsel. Aligning with truth distinguishes between those who use transparency to manipulate and those who submit in vulnerability to live lives of integrity.

Figure 7.1. The Third Rung of the Character Ladder

In the example given in Chapter Six (Bruce's five friends opposing his board nomination), what would have happened if, after going to them in vulnerability and listening to their counsel, he had then pushed ahead, trying to get around their objections? But he didn't. He listened intently and looked for the wisdom in their words. Although their critique stung at first, his decision to yield to their counsel had far-reaching results. Those friends now receive Bruce's advice and counsel in their deepest struggles. Why? Because vulnerability expresses our heart's desire to live with integrity. And the resulting realignment of our lives convinces others of our commitment to adhere to the truth. Seeing this, people will come to trust us to influence them in ways they never would have before.

The climb up the character ladder is a climb toward interdependence. No matter how much people try to romanticize or idolize the self-protective isolation of many leaders, lovers, entrepreneurs, and artists, they would be better served by choosing to live and work in community. Frederick Buechner eloquently describes this reciprocal dynamic.

> We hunger to be known and understood. We hunger to be loved. We hunger to be at peace inside our own skins. We hunger not just to be fed these things but, often without realizing it, we hunger to feed others these things because they too are starving for them. We hunger not just to be loved but to love, not just to be forgiven but to forgive, not just to be known and understood for all the good times and bad times that for better or worse have made us who we are, but to know and understand each other to the point of seeing that, in the last analysis, we all have the same good times, the same bad times, and that for that very reason there is no such thing in all the world as anyone who is really a stranger.
>
> When Jesus commanded us to love our neighbors as ourselves, it was not just for our neighbors' sakes that he commanded it, but for our own sakes as well.[3]

To align ourselves with truth is a personal decision that is best made in a community of people who care for us. The truth about who we are cannot be wholly known without interaction with others. We all have blind spots that others have to help us with.

The Johari window, developed by Joe Luft and Harry Ingham, provides a more serious illustration of how others can help us with our blind spots (see Figure 7.2). We all have parts of our lives that are known to others and parts that remain unknown. Our lives also have parts that are known to us and other parts that are unknown to us. The perceptions of others can help us see the areas where we are blind. Much of what they see—that we can't—has to do with our character.

Figure 7.2. The Effect of Vulnerability on the Johari Window

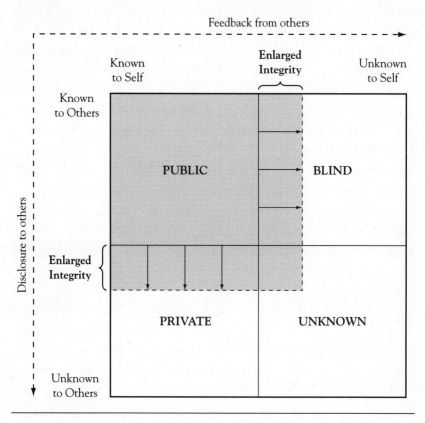

Source: Adapted from Hersey and Blanchard, 1993, p. 299.

Although many capacities can be developed outside of intimate, authentic relationships, *character cannot*. We need others to look into our lives and tell us the truth. We need them to challenge us, encourage us, and most of all help us embrace the truth about us. We need community—a concept that Westerners may overlook in our preoccupation with the individual.

Upper and Lower Stories

In Hebrew philosophy, a belief was not a belief until it was acted on. And all beliefs affected community, because the actions they spawned affected every area of life. In Greek philosophy, belief could be separated from action. Thought and action suffered a painful divorce into upper and lower levels of existence.

The material world—the realm of the senses and action—declined in value. The spiritual world—the realm of the mind and emotions—represented a higher plane of existence. The work of earning daily bread played second fiddle to the loftier mental pursuit of philosophy. This thinking still pervades modern thought in a variety of ways.

Hebrew philosophy seems comparatively simple; there is no separation between thought and action. If you love a person, you will meet that person's need. If you meet someone's need, you love them. The Hebrews did not separate the heart from the mind, or belief from action. What you believed affected all you did, from cooking a meal to building a city. Therefore no vocation was viewed as higher than another.

To say we have chosen to align our lives with truth while remaining isolated and invulnerable from the guidance and love of others puts our destiny in jeopardy.

How does all this relate to the character ladder? First, when we merge our doing with our being, we recognize how important every area of life is and how integrated each step of the ladder is. There can be no true humility—trusting God with me—without an act of vulnerability. There can be no vulnerability without a corresponding alignment with truth.

Second, there is no room for an isolated existence. Each step of the ladder requires application in the context of relationship. We cannot trust God or others, choose vulnerability, or align with truth without relationships. They will instead become cheap, intellectual exercises providing little benefit to ourselves or others.

To say we have chosen to align our lives with truth while remaining isolated and invulnerable from the guidance and love of others puts our destiny in jeopardy. But there is a profoundly beautiful antidote created by God for us. Entering into relationships of trust, coming under the influence of others, and then following through on what they say opens us up to God's best for our lives.

Obedience Versus Compliance

In addition to dualistic thinking, there is another hazard we face on the third rung, stemming from a subtle misunderstanding of alignment. We may think that complying with the demands of others is the same as obedience. But *obedience* is a heart word describing not just our actions but our attitudes. Compliance sounds like, "OK, OK. I'll do it. But it won't be pretty. I'll do it, but this story is not over. Someone, sometime, somewhere, is gonna pay." Obedience from the heart says, "I'll do this because I trust you and believe it is for our best." Aligning with truth flows from a heart that obeys in trust. Compliance simply concedes to the oppression of an unhealthy environment. Compliance, even when it takes the form of serving others, typically harbors some form of rebellion or resentment. Obedience from the heart, on the other hand, develops trust and acceptance.

It may sound to some people as though the obedience implied in alignment with truth excuses them from personal responsibility, because they are simply doing what others ask or tell them to. Compliant people tend to hide behind the choices others make for their lives. Alignment with truth means nothing of the sort. Obedience is facing our responsibility, our needs, our ambitions, our choices, our attitudes and actions with ruthless honesty. It is a heart-choice to pursue the freedom of truth in the context of community.

Flame of Glory

Another obstacle often causes people to slip from the third rung. We call it the "flame of glory" syndrome. It stems from lack of hope or from fear of being controlled. Convinced that they cannot handle the counsel of others, they cannot change themselves, or they cannot change their environment, they trade the possibilities of the future for what can be experienced in the present moment. They may go wild in their pursuit of pleasure or settle for subtler forms of surrender: "I just want to be happy. Can't I just leave here and start over somewhere else? Perhaps a new relationship or new job is the ticket?" Someone who has found success on the capacity ladder may fall victim to indifference, saying something like, "Who needs character or this relationship stuff? I've got it made on the capacity ladder."

But remember, the person at the top who has pursued his or her own exaltation is a different person than the one at the start of the journey. Whatever that perch promised always, always, always disappoints when you arrive. Because, as Solomon learned, joy and delight and contentment and the ability to experience the beauty of "arriving" are all gifts from God's hand, enjoyed only by those who choose his ladder.

We're ready for the next rung.

Grabbing Hold

- With whom do you intentionally share your needs? Which relationships have helped you mature?

- In what ways have you ignored advice that could have helped you?

- Which heart attitude dominates your choices: obedience from the heart or compliance?

- Do you encourage obedience or compliance in your leadership?

Chapter Eight

The Fourth Rung

Paying the Price

Courage is not the absence of fear, but rather the
judgment that something else is more important
than fear.

—*Ambrose Redmoon*

Responding to adversity is the supreme test of the fourth rung. One
young woman responded exceedingly well when she encountered
unfairness in the form of sexual discrimination back in 1952. In
those days, few firms hired woman attorneys, and they weren't
about to change their practices for her, despite her Stanford degree.
Her painful circumstances forced a decision early in her career. She
suffered from other people's wrong choices and, ultimately, from a
culture that tolerated and even encouraged such discrimination. In
response, she started her own law practice, taking on many cases
the other firms wouldn't touch. And this choice led to its own
painful trials. But she pressed on in faith.

She had earned a well-deserved reputation for fairness,
integrity, and honesty as a lawyer when in 1965 she became assis-
tant attorney general for her state. Four years later, the governor
appointed her to a vacated state senate seat, which she then won
in her own right in 1972. Soon she was elected as state senate
majority leader; she was the first woman in the United States to
hold such a position. But her first love was law. So she faced
another fourth-rung decision. Aligning with the truth about who
she was, she chose to let go of political power and switch to the

judicial branch of government in 1974, winning a county superior court seat.

By 1978, public figures and political contacts began to urge her to run for governor. She knew that winning such a position would offer the power to positively influence a much larger constituency. She faced another choice.

Privately, she discussed her options among a group of advisers. She heard their counsel. She compared it with what she knew about who she was—lessons learned from over twenty years of consistent use of the character ladder. When she emerged from the process, she had made her decision. She would not run. She had no idea whether she would ever have such an opportunity again. She couldn't have known what would happen next. She chose not to pursue power, willing to pay the price of letting go of such an opportunity.

In this case, she went on to receive far greater influence than she could have hoped for. Soon a committee appointed her to the state court of appeals. Then, in 1981, President Reagan nominated this woman—Sandra Day O'Connor—for appointment to the U.S. Supreme Court. On September 22, 1981, a clear majority confirmed the first woman to serve on the high court.

We can look at stories like this and assume that fourth-rung choices will lead to such benefits for us. We may view the character ladder as the means to a capacity goal. But this is vanity. Paying the price can never be about winning in the short term—about competing or proving ourselves against others. It's about something beyond winning. It's about reaching our destiny by entrusting it into the capable hands of God.

Fourth-Rung Fears

On the capacity ladder, our strengths, training, experiences, and titles may have carried us to the fourth rung. Getting to the fourth rung on the short ladder is arriving at the top. In contrast, getting to the fourth rung on the character ladder means we still face some of the toughest challenges.

On the fourth rung of the *capacity* ladder, we may enjoy certain recognition, privileges, power, and authority from our climb. On the fourth rung of the *character* ladder, we come face to face with what is inside us. At this level, we find daily opportunities to set aside those same short-ladder payoffs in order to make profound differences in the lives of others.

But we also find a more-than-coincidental increase in "short-ladder-payoff" opportunities if we simply back off on a character issue or two. What's so hard is that the option to back off does not come in an obvious, easy form, like choosing between committing an armed robbery or cleaning out the garage. It comes in a form that may be obvious *only to you*. The temptation to "modify" your values may appear to have the power to speed you on in your destiny, while the choice of integrity may bring delay, setback, or the end of a dream. Oh, and by the way, this "opportunity" will usually come in the form of something you've desperately felt would make your life complete, *if only you could get it*.

This is a scary intersection because it puts to the test what you really believe about how life works. Are you all alone in a random world of coincidence, where blind chance flashes opportunity onto the screen for just a moment and if you don't snatch it someone else will? Is this how life works? If so, you must protect yourself and exploit every opportunity, whether or not it violates, because you have no idea if it will come your way again. *Or* could it be that there's a God out there who knows your name and cares about you more than you care about you? And is he fully capable of getting you where he knows is best for you? Is maybe *that* how life works? Well then, my friend, now you're playing Black Jack in a casino where the dealer is showing all his cards. All you have to do is concern yourself with doing right and entrust yourself to someone who carries all the aces. This is the test of rung four.

A student nearing graduation, realizing that her heart is moving in a different direction from her major, may have to make some tough choices about her education. A father may need to cut back on work hours to care for his spouse or family, hurting his chances for a promotion or even jeopardizing his job. A woman who finds that she has chosen the wrong profession for the wrong reasons may find it difficult to sacrifice her current status in order to enter a new phase of personal growth, even if her newfound discovery appears exciting and more aligned with the truth about who she is. This tension creates tremendous pressure to step off the long ladder—to kick back and rest a while. Or, if we attempt the climb, we may freeze from fear as we see what lies ahead.

Those at the top of the capacity ladder face the greatest potential pain or loss in honoring the process of climbing the character ladder. They simply have more to lose than those on the lower capacity rungs.

It's on the fourth rung of both ladders that we face the greatest challenges from without. Subordinates or coworkers who covet power or position may use our weaknesses against us. It's also on the fourth rungs that we face the greatest challenges from within. Will I use my gifts, strengths, or power simply to hold on to my position? My privileges? My paycheck? Will I hide who I am in order to fool those around me? My friends? My spouse? My team? My coworkers?

Sieges of the Heart

The song "Healing Touch" once profoundly helped Ken see his own depression:

> I stare at the door, trapped in a dream
> Held like a captive
> By what people see on the outside
> They don't really know me

Trapped. Held like a captive. Unknown. You might be surprised by how many people feel the same way, especially those who have made it to the top of the capacity ladder. But then again, maybe not. Maybe you have been there or are there now. In Ken's case, he had pursued a path toward a goal. But when he reached the goal, he found he had given up too much of what really mattered in order to attain it. He found himself gripped with fear.

> *Shades of the truth locked up in lies*
> *Days run into days*
> *When I open my eyes, see how far it's gone*
> *Where did things go wrong?*
> *Choices were made, dreams were pushed aside*
> *Not so much a conscious thought*
> *But resignation, a siege of the heart*
> *But there's a part that calls to You*

Where did things go wrong? What are those things that we sometimes resign ourselves to—those "sieges of the heart" that can rob us of our dreams and our destiny? There are many.

- We may subtly shift our emphasis from what's best for those around us to what's best for our ego. (Dennis Miller says, "We all know that the ego is the ugly little troll that lives underneath the bridge between your mind and your heart, and power is the nutritional source that feeds the ego.")[1]
- We may succumb to the myth of arrival, confusing our capacity goals with our ultimate destiny, leading us into arrogance. ("I may have my faults," reads the tag line on the poster featuring a rhinoceros, "but being wrong isn't one of them.")
- We begin to believe we are "special," that we cannot be understood by anyone except those in some clique or club that just affirms our wrong assumptions. (This leads to Ashleigh Brilliant's dilemma, "How can I prove I'm not crazy to people who are?")[2]

Each of these temptations can keep us frozen at this rung of the character ladder and drive us further and further into isolation. Still, as the lyric says, amid these sieges there is always that "part that calls to You." We still have hope because God's grace can lead us home.

The Price of Love

Relationships and environments of grace call for people who are willing to pay the price to earn trust. "Men of genius are admired. Men of wealth are envied. Men of power are feared," Arthur Friedman once said, "but only men of character are trusted."[3]

Trusted leaders are leaders who have the ability to love. Yet, to experience the benefits of love, we must receive love. For love to be received, the receiver must trust the giver. To be trusted, the giver must have integrity. To have integrity, the giver must submit to others in vulnerability and align with truth in obedience. At the bottom of all this, givers of love must entrust themselves to God in humility. We know this is a lot of concepts to process, but the bottom line is that love only grows in the soil of trust.

This pattern can be seen clearly in the life of Jesus,

> who had equal status with God but didn't think so much of himself that he had to cling to the advantages of that status no matter what. Not at all. When the time came, he set aside the privileges of deity and took on the status of a slave, became *human!* And having become human, he *stayed* human. It was an incredibly humbling process. He didn't claim special privileges. Instead, he lived a selfless, obedient life.[4]

So far, so good. We may even be encouraged by what followed Jesus' obedience: "God lifted him high and honored him far beyond anyone or anything, ever."[5] Now *that's* getting to the top of the ladder!

Did you notice that we left out one small but important phrase that came between "pay the price" and "discover my destiny"? What kind of price did Jesus pay? He "died a selfless, obedient death—and the worst kind of death at that: a crucifixion."[6] Jesus, the best example of a servant leader, paid the ultimate price in order to express God's love to others. On the character ladder, we all must pay a price. Within the boundaries of loving God and loving others, the payment will be different for each of us. God does not have the same plan for everyone.

Jesus shows just how varied the price can be. When a man named Zacchaeus decided to use a portion of his great wealth to repay what he had cheated from others, Jesus affirmed him.[7] But Jesus commanded another rich man to sell everything he had and give it to the poor.[8] Jesus asked some people to follow him by leaving their homes and careers behind. Others Jesus told to return to their home towns, despite their pleadings to be allowed to follow him. Some of Jesus' followers lived to a ripe old age. Others died young as martyrs. It would be much easier to count the cost of aligning with truth if we all walked the same path. But we don't.

> *For love to be received, the receiver must trust the giver. To be trusted, the giver must have integrity. To have integrity, the giver must submit to others in vulnerability and align with truth in obedience.*

Some will be asked to pay the price of living in obscurity while they devote themselves to the service of others, when a different choice could have brought them fame or fortune. Others will be asked to use their athletic gifts and pay the price of living continuously under the glare of the spotlight. Make no mistake about it; there will be a price to pay when we choose to climb the character ladder to the point of aligning with truth. This is why the fourth rung can leave us paralyzed partway up this longer ladder. *Pay the price* implies something that none of us likes to think about. It implies suffering (see Figure 8.1).

We need trusted friends here, on this fourth rung, maybe more than at any other place on the ladder. Because, as we said, this is at

Figure 8.1. The Fourth Rung of the Character Ladder

times a frightening, lonely place, where everything we say we believe is being sifted. Trusted friends who know us and share our values can help us evaluate the costs of our decisions, reminding us of the goal of our climb. Concerned, committed friends who tell us the truth can restore our objectivity—our ability to remain focused on reality. Without objectivity, we may react to a situation based on pain from our past, the crisis of the moment, or fear of the future. We are left with the empty bravado of the cartoon character who says, "I can face anything, except the future, and certain parts of the past and present."

Two Starting Points

There are two basic starting points for regaining objectivity. We can begin with failure or we can begin with truth. The process typically goes faster and requires less pain when we head down the "truth" road. But because this path requires that we trust God, trust others, and choose vulnerability, many of us end up on the longer, winding, road of failure on our way to objectivity. Either route can get us to our destination if we can survive the trip. If we refuse to hear and obey the truth, by default we have chosen the road of failure. The key to survival on this more dangerous path is to embrace the lessons failure teaches. When we allow failure to teach us humility, for instance, we discover a shortcut back to the road of truth.

There are two basic starting points for regaining objectivity. We can begin with failure or we can begin with truth. The process typically goes faster and requires less pain when we head down the "truth" road.

Several years ago, Bruce interviewed a successful medical professional who had been caught in a lie. For years, the woman had anesthetized her emotional pain by becoming addicted to drugs. At first, she stole a few pain pills from the medical supply cabinet at work. Then she began raiding the cabinet more often, until finally someone got suspicious and caught her. Only after getting caught did she realize how far she'd gone.

Bruce asked her if it would have been helpful to have someone confront her or at least take an interest in her life during that time. She said, "No. I was so convinced I could make certain choices and not suffer. No amount of insight would have helped me." When asked what would have helped, she answered very quickly and succinctly: "I think I needed a crisis. I needed to lose my practice, almost lose my husband, have my errors made public, and have to acknowledge my wrongs before I finally could see clearly and admit my behavior."

Do we all need a crisis to snap us out of our stupor? The medical professional's experience reveals that indeed we sometimes have to fail, or at least face impending failure, before we are willing to hear the truth from God and others.

But there is another way.

Encouraging Words

We cannot promise you that the final rungs will be easy. They will not be. But "easy" is overrated. There is a cartoon about playing golf in heaven that shows a golfer on a green standing over a putt. Everything's normal about the picture except that the hole is about ten feet wide. And we think, "Now that's heaven!" But is it? How much fun would it be if everyone could shoot a birdie every time? After about five rounds of easy, most of us would look around for something else to do. Fun is growing your skills enough to birdie on a challenging hole more often than you ever have. Easy isn't the ticket. But throughout the process, we know that at the controls is one who never has to say "Oops." He has seen the end from the beginning, and he is more concerned about our welfare and destiny than we ever could on our best day. That's a fact. And we can rest assured that there will be many other hands to help us if we've committed ourselves to the first three rungs.

Let us encourage you with these truths before we move on. First, God can be trusted to stand by and support the humble and help them up the rungs of the character ladder in due time.[9] Second, many others have gone before you and made it. You are not alone in your ascent. Third, if you recall what you've learned along the way, choosing to lean heavily on the lower rungs and finding strength in the relationship and environment rails, you will be able to endure the testing of "paying the price."

Grabbing Hold

- What significant challenges are you facing on the character ladder?
- Who gets your best?
- What do you think hinders leaders from "paying the price"?
- If you were losing your objectivity, how would you reclaim it?

Chapter Nine

The Fifth Rung

Discovering Your Destiny

> None of us knows what the next change is going to
> be, what unexpected opportunity is just around the
> corner, waiting a few months or a few years to
> change all the tenor of our lives.
>
> —*Kathleen Norris*

Parker swallowed hard as the Quaker's question hit him in the heart: "What would you like most about being a president?" He had gathered this group of trusted friends—a Quaker clearness committee—to simply ask him questions, helping him sort out an invitation to become president of an educational institution.

Years earlier, at the age of twenty-nine, Parker Palmer had been invited to become the only member of the board of trustees under sixty at a major educational institution. The president made the prediction that someday Palmer would be president of a college and that serving on the board of trustees would be part of his training.

A search for his destiny had led the aspiring sociologist to Pendle Hill, a Quaker community committed to educating people about the inner journey and nonviolent social change. As dean there, Palmer had learned much about a new approach to education and teaching, rooted in community. However, his aspirations were larger, and he was sure that his destiny lay beyond this obscure Quaker community; perhaps he could become president of a major college as earlier predicted.

After what seemed an eternity, Parker finally begins to utter an answer to this seemingly simple question.

> Well, I would not like having to give up my writing and teaching. I would not like the politics and having to glad hand people simply because they have money. . . . I would not like. . . . I would not like having to give up my summer vacations or having to wear a suit. . . . I would not like. . . .

A gentle reminder interrupted the litany of negatives: "May I remind you that the question was, "What would you like most?""

Parker Palmer was trapped into this honest response by people he had gathered to impress with his invitation. In his words:

> But this time I felt compelled to give the only honest answer I possessed, an answer that came from the very bottom of my barrel, an answer that appalled even me as I spoke it. "Well," said I, in the smallest voice I possess, "I guess what I'd like most is getting my picture in the paper with the word *president* under it."

As he recounts, his seasoned Quaker questioners sat silent for minutes as the absurdity of his own answer did surgery on Palmer's enlarged ego. Finally, the sage who'd posed the penetrating question loosed the pent-up laughter with the final question of the evening, "Can you think of an easier way to get your picture in the paper?"[1]

All of us long for the fifth rung. In our hearts, whether we aspire to large or small dreams, we hope to leave an enduring legacy for our children, our organizations, or even our world. We want to live life as God intended and live it well. We want to find and fulfill our destiny. But what real hope do we have? How do we get on and stay on the fifth rung?

The Surprising Fifth Rung

As Parker Palmer learned the hard way, the fifth rung cannot be grabbed. All the other rungs of the character ladder present definitive steps of action. There, we must make intentional, operative choices. But fifth-rungers seem lifted there by some unseen force. They seem to be drawn onto it. Rather than representing an intentional step up from the fourth rung, this fifth step—*discover my destiny*—appears to be more passive, as if it "just happens." But appearances can be deceiving (see Figure 9.1).

When Christopher Columbus set out to find a passage to India, he made great preparations for the trip. He had a goal and a plan, and he worked hard to secure the means. In the process, he discovered far more than he imagined possible—a whole new world. Discovering destiny can be like this. We make intentional choices on the first four rungs; these choices and their consequences serve as

Figure 9.1. The Fifth Rung of the Character Ladder

intense preparation for what lies ahead. But when we reach the fifth rung, we may be surprised by a destiny far beyond our expectations.

Parker Palmer did discover his destiny. He continued his educational development at Pendle Hill for many years, discovering his true gifts as an educational theorist and writer. He was lifted to the fifth rung by his influence on teachers and students. Left to himself, he would have become the frustrated president of a struggling institution. But he had done the preparation by climbing the character ladder and learning the importance of humility and vulnerability. By trusting God and his community, Palmer was lifted to a place of influence that had an impact on many colleges and educational leaders. In 1998, he was named one of the thirty most influential senior leaders in higher education by the American Association for Higher Education. And he never did get a picture in the paper with the word *president* under it.

Historical Examples

What do other fifth-rung people look like? One could choose from many examples, but let's consider two people from back in 1947— a good year for the long ladder—to get an idea. One was a small, frail woman; the other a tall, impressive man. One expressed overtly religious views; the other held his faith more privately. Yet both possessed tremendous inner strength and a power plainly evident to others. The similarities in their leadership and life purpose and in the development of their inner life are even more striking.

Power Amid Poverty

The first is Mary Teresa Bojaxhiu, who, from the time she was eighteen, knew without a doubt that her life would be different. Twenty years later, in 1947, she founded the Missionaries of Charity and began working with the poorest of the poor in Calcutta. Only after another twenty years of relative obscurity would Mary, who became known as Mother Teresa, begin to be noticed by outsiders. Her devotion to the poor earned her the respect and support of virtually everyone.

The power of her mission and the force of her personality surmounted political roadblocks. She was as comfortable asking Ronald Reagan for assistance in feeding Ethiopians as she was soliciting the Marxist-atheist leader of West Bengal. She didn't pursue power, but she certainly wielded a lot, through her worldwide recognition, audiences with world leaders, and honorary doctorates; she was even awarded the Nobel Peace Prize. Still, her humility remained evident. She would only accept the Nobel award on behalf of the poor, requesting that the award dinner be canceled (which it was) and the money be used to feed and house the destitute and dying.

Before her death, someone called this small, deeply lined, and quiet woman "the most powerful woman in the world." When told of this remark, she responded, "I wish I was. Then I could bring peace to the world."[2] But back in 1947, this task fell to others, among them a man named George Catlin Marshall.

Marshalling Peace

In 1947, General Marshall began his duties as U.S. secretary of state. Soon after, this man, now "fourth-fifths forgotten," according to his children, somehow pulled off a miracle through what would become known as the Marshall Plan.

Marshall had seen firsthand the starving masses of Europeans, the growing anger of an embattled continent, and the breakdown of order following a horrible war. He took immediate action to rebuild a war-torn world. Putting his reputation and his job on the line, he made a brief but compelling speech while accepting an honorary doctorate from Harvard.

His speech surprised President Truman, sent shock waves around the world, and galvanized the nation. Did he really believe the nations of Europe could collaborate on such a large scale after two wars? Could he, unlike Stalin, truly renounce any self-interested aims, especially when Europe was ripe for the picking? Did he really believe the most powerful nation on earth would use its power for Europe's protection and not conquest?

Yes, he believed that! Everyone who knew Marshall understood that he was simply extending his own personal beliefs into the arena of foreign policy. Those beliefs included setting aside the rights of position for the benefit of others, serving others with excellence, and sharing power with those who were powerless.

The plan worked, primarily because Marshall assumed the role of a servant leader, working tirelessly to win the support of the American people and Congress on behalf of Europe. Far beyond Marshall's hopes, the Europeans learned to cooperate out of necessity and so established the framework for the current political structure of the free world, including NATO. Marshall's leadership can be credited with protecting freedom, saving perhaps millions of lives, and rebuilding war-torn countries to take their place in a new, global economy. Like Mother Teresa, he too received the Nobel Peace Prize—the only military person ever to do so.[3]

At the time, many, including Harry Truman and Winston Churchill, believed George Marshall to be the most powerful man in the world. They were probably right.

The Ladder That Goes Way Up

Although George Marshall and Mary Teresa Bojaxhiu shared similar goals in 1947—feeding the hungry, working for world peace, and committing their lives to a higher purpose—their positions and organizations could not have been more different. The character ladder works as well for the poor as for the rich, for the politically impoverished as for the politically powerful, for volunteer organizations as for the military. We find people of character and thus of tremendous influence in all walks of life, young and old. Spiritual power is available to all who climb to the top of the character ladder. So how did Mother Teresa and General Marshall get to the fifth rung?

Their respective paths reveal much about the short (capacity) and the long (character) ladders they both climbed. The choice between the short ladder and the long ladder is not an either-or decision; it is a both-and decision. They are long-lost friends, once again realizing how much they need each other. To climb both ladders represents the only reasonable way to rise to positions of influence with character intact. To reject this integration is to reject reality and growth.

For instance, Marshall rose through the military ranks because he served well, accepting and excelling at increasingly complicated leadership tasks. Mother Teresa had her own short ladder to climb before she could gain permission to embark on her mission. Neither rose to world prominence until later in life—in their sixties—after years of relative obscurity. Both endured numerous setbacks and embraced many opportunities for the long-ladder process to take root.

Both of them integrated the rungs of the capacity ladder with the rungs of the character ladder. They did this by using the only rails that can bring character and capacity together: they found healthy relationships of trust and environments of grace that honored their capacities while nurturing their characters.

Here we make a fascinating discovery. We can apply the strong rails of relationships of trust and environments of grace from the character ladder to the shaky rails of the capacity ladder. As illustrated in Figure 9.2, the character ladder can function as an extension, expanding our capacities far beyond what they would have been without character. Character is what protects and leverages the gifts of your talents, temperament, and training. This is where it gets really great, when we can integrate the ladders. That's the goal, isn't it—not to lose capacity but to wonderfully extend capacity by bringing character to it? Ordinary people in ordinary relationships can do extraordinary things with such an integrated ladder.

Figure 9.2. The Integration of the Character
and Capacity Ladders

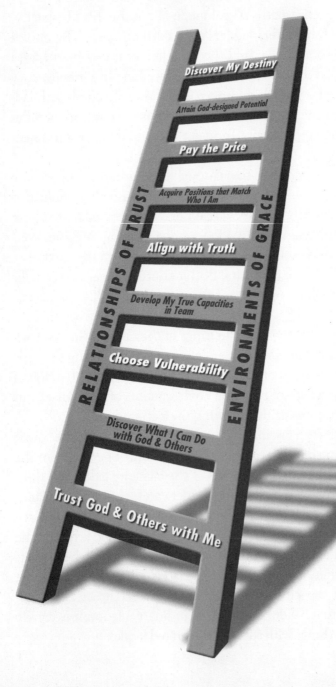

The lives of Marshall and Mother Teresa confirm this. While ascending the capacity ladder, they made a bunch of difficult choices—intentional choices—that developed and honed their character in relationships. For instance, after graduating as a young man from the Virginia Military Institute, the young Marshall chose to remain committed and faithful to his first wife, even after she surprised him on their honeymoon night with devastating news: she had a heart condition that would prevent them from ever consummating their marriage. Mother Teresa chose to endure the critiques, rejections, and arduous approval process needed to form her new order. She could have struck out on her own, but she chose instead to remain committed to the church and the people she trusted, long before they trusted her.

The General and the Nun

How did these two amazing people rise to the fifth rung? The general and the nun, who both possessed power and clout, earned it by putting others first. For instance, Marshall, amid a political firestorm, chose to remain silent rather than lobby on his own behalf for the chief of staff position. Despite Marshall's inferior rank and Douglas MacArthur's efforts to the contrary, Franklin Roosevelt chose Marshall, much to the dismay of three senior generals who had vied for the title. Marshall himself tried to talk Roosevelt out of it, concerned that others might be more qualified by rank.

Mother Teresa repeatedly turned down opportunities for publicity and personal gain. Still, many leaders visited her and sought her counsel, including Princess Diana, who attributed her devotion to humanitarian causes to the influence of Mother Teresa. Mother Teresa's life of self-sacrifice and devotion to the poor stirs something deep within all of us. It wasn't her personal power or charisma that drew us. We see something in her that beckons us to become more than we are. All she longed for was to be the hands and feet of Jesus. Maybe that's what we saw. Maybe that's what causes us to want to be like her in some way.

Some people have a way of raising the bar by setting an example that encourages us to believe we too can do great things. In 1954, Roger Bannister became the first human to break the four-minute-mile barrier. What's more amazing, as Harvey Mackay points out, is that the following year thirty-seven others ran sub-four miles. And the year after that, over three hundred more men did it.[4]

Now here's the God part. Behind the veil, from before time, God has prepared the exact timing of destiny's discovery. He's more faithful than *Old* Faithful. He cannot be coerced to speed it up or slow it down. The God who knows and loves you will not be bullied or moved by whining or threats. We can't rush this destiny. We typically cannot even imagine it. God takes the initiative to lift us up when he chooses. The Hebrew-Christian tradition speaks often of this occurrence. In the Psalms we are told, "No one from the east or the west or from the desert can exalt a man. But it is God who judges: He brings one down, he exalts another."[5] Jesus said, "Whoever exalts himself will be humbled, and whoever humbles himself will be exalted."[6] And the apostle Peter once told aspiring fifth-rungers, "Humble yourselves, therefore, under God's mighty hand, that he may lift you up in due time."[7] As M. Scott Peck wrote in *A World Waiting to Be Born:*

> Increasingly, the civil leader or manager begins to sense that the power of her position is not hers. It is not her possession; it is not hers to possess. The power belongs to God, and the proper role of the civil leader is merely to be a conduit and to steward that power as God's agent. Merely! What a paradox! To exercise temporal power with civility is to undertake a role of great glory, and it can only be undertaken with genuine humility.[8]

When we examine the natural talents of great influencers, we often find little that distinguishes them. But when we look at their character, we find the essential ingredients of greatness. They trusted God and others. They chose vulnerability. They aligned with truth and paid the price for their decisions. God then elevated these prepared people to positions of honor and influence beyond their potential apart from their character.

Don't Plan It But Don't Miss It: Some Fifth-Rung Challenges

Getting to and staying on the fifth rung has nothing to do with pursuing power. It is about learning *how to receive power.* We can't plan it. In fact, we shouldn't even try to plan it. But we certainly don't want to miss it either. Therefore, we must prepare. Here are a few challenges that we must plan on facing as we seek to plant ourselves on the fifth rung.

Getting to and staying on the fifth rung has nothing to do with pursuing power. It is about learning how to receive power.

First, *we must continue to change and grow while facing increasing pressure to mentor others.* Change and growth require teachability. To remain teachable, we must let go of our pride and let others speak into our lives. We must cultivate a growing sense of interdependency. Our character may give us increasing opportunities to teach and mentor others. This means we may get less done in the present, but we will actually accomplish far more in the future by pouring our lives into the lives of others who can devote themselves to the causes that are nearest to our hearts.

The willingness to remain teachable and to be taught stems from the commitment to interdependency. No matter how much we mature, character weaknesses and unresolved issues will still surface throughout our lives. It's as if our hearts are like a dark room with a shaded window. Early in life, God only allows the shade to go up a little to reveal things that must be dealt with on our way up the character ladder. As we mature, God raises the shade a bit further, based on what we can handle amid our current environment and relationships. God never just throws up the shade completely, revealing all our issues at once. We couldn't handle it. It would devastate us. But to remain on the fifth rung, we must continue to resolve the issues God *does* allow us to see.

We can only do this in the context of a culture of grace, where relationships and environment converge to create the safety and acceptance needed to address the issues of our hearts. When we commit ourselves to this process, it can feel fragile at times because the vulnerability of interdependence becomes our new path to the accomplishment of anything significant.

If you want to know whether you are on the fifth rung, it is to your community you must turn. Personal intuition or running away to a desert has little value in this matter. Instead, ask your friends. Ask your community. They'll tell you, if you let them. In fact, this is the truest test of discovering destiny—when those you influence acknowledge God's hand in elevating you, despite their knowledge of your weaknesses.

Second, *we must express both compassion and conviction by actively seeking new opportunities to serve others*. For fifth-rung climbers, this involves an ever-expanding search for ways to care for and improve the circumstances of others. We must continually seek ways to integrate our hearts with our hands, our daily lives with our dreams, and our capacities with our character. This may feel like the toughest challenge of all.

After all these years, I get to the fifth rung, and I now want to spend some of the currency of my character-ladder choices. I might be tempted to feel I've earned the right to take care of me for awhile. But the same lifestyle that brought me there, the same heart and way of seeing doesn't change when he brings me to my destiny. Continuing to look outward and live for the needs of others feels filled with risk. I'll ask these questions more than once:

Am I losing out? Am I playing the fool, giving when I should be getting? I look around me and I see others in similar areas of influence
seemingly getting ahead. Am I falling behind? Am I wasting my
talents that could move me along in such a greater way if I paid more
attention to self-promotion?

Again we're brought face to face with what we believe about how
this life is run. If it is a random universe, then it must be all about you
protecting you and exploiting every opportunity to catch every ring.
And we will be able to offer only the *appearance of sacrificial giving*.
But if there is a God who is in control of your life, as he claims, then
we must place our destiny fully into his hands. We must refuse to
measure it by comparing our sphere of influence to that of others.

We can't tell a fifth-runger solely by breadth of influence or
height of position. This is how we know: in positions of influence,
however great or small, they retain a character-ladder perspective on
life. They will not pursue their potential at the expense of conviction and character. They will look to God and their community—
not their own evaluation—to affirm their influence.

We all know of celebrities or leaders who make it to the top of
a profession or community, only to make the mistake of moving forward without those who brought them there. The third challenge
is to choose to benefit our friends, team, and community rather
than just benefiting *from* them. No one rises to the fifth rung in isolation. Yet some decide to derive an exclusively personal benefit
from the sacrifices that others have made for them. For instance,
pastors may teach and be taught within an intimate community for
years and then succumb to the deception that they can capitalize
on their team's success without sharing the rewards. Artists may
enjoy personal success without acknowledging those who helped
and supported them along the way. But mature fifth-rungers find
creative ways to share the joys, recognition, and benefits with those
around them. This keeps their own importance in proper perspective and helps others enjoy the fruit of their faithfulness.

"Sacrifices in the service of callings take many forms," writes Gregg Levoy in his book, CALLINGS: *Finding and Following an Authentic Life*. His list of possible sacrifices includes the following:

- In order to share your work with the world, you will have to yield some privacy.
- If you want to collaborate with others, you will need to share power, which can be a stinker because you also have to let go of control.
- In order to help loved ones, you may need to let go of trying to rescue them.
- To focus on a creative project, you necessarily must set aside other commitments.

But it is the last item that is particularly poignant:

If you feel compelled to create a healthy relationship, you may need to sacrifice time that you might have spent building your career, time that you may not be able to make up but that may present you with the lesser of two regrets in the end. Though power tends to win in the struggle between power and love, love tends to have the last word. J. Paul Getty, who sacrificed his marriages on the altar of power and prosperity, said this late in life: "I hate and regret the failure of my marriages. I would gladly give all my millions for just one lasting marital success." He wouldn't, of course, while he was busy *making* those millions, but priorities naturally change as we get older, and it's easier to see our sacrifices for what they were.[9]

Fifth-Rung Realities

How can we know if we have reached the fifth rung? We can never tell by title, power, or position because these can be deceptive.

We know a retired high school history teacher who leads from the fifth rung. Chuck is nearly eighty now, and he often falls asleep in church. A round of golf for him is more of a nice walk with a friend, occasionally interrupted by a ball in his path, which he must swat away with a stick. But the man exudes peace, contentment, and grace. Hang out with Chuck for five minutes and you can't help but be encouraged. He doesn't even have to say anything. Yet his influence is penetrating. You'd become a better person just by watching the man garden. Many speak of the life-shaping difference this unassuming man has made in their lives.

> *Though power tends to win in the struggle between power and love, love tends to have the last word.*
>
> —GREGG LEVOY

You probably won't get a chance to meet Chuck before his days on earth are through. But if you did, you would probably wonder how such a man, who seems so, for lack of a better word, normal, can exude such strength, honesty, and vulnerability. The answer is that he has discovered his destiny, receiving it from the hand of God: a penetrating influence that affects everyone around him. Mother Teresa and George Marshall may seem like examples beyond your reach. But we can all become like Chuck, a simple person of profound love and trust. We can all discover our destiny.

As we have said, "You cannot plan your destiny, but you can prepare for it." To discover your destiny and remain on the fifth rung, you must not avoid those three challenges. Facing them will bring you closer to extraordinary influence—the kind that provides the greatest contributions to the common good. Indeed, the hope of our world hangs in the balance. What the world needs most are fifth-rung people who, like Mary Teresa, George, and Chuck, will pay the costs and reap the rewards of finding and fulfilling their destinies. In so doing, they will become people of influence, which is what the next chapter is all about.

Grabbing Hold

- Are you in a process that is helping you discover your destiny? If not, what steps are necessary to enter that process?
- Do you value servant leadership?
- What part do you think God plays in shaping your destiny?
- Which of the seven challenges have you encountered? Which have you refused to accept?
- For you, is discovering your destiny worth the risks? If not, where is the disconnect?
- How have you benefited from another person's fifth-rung experiences?

Chapter Ten

Discovering Beautiful Influence

Let them remember there is meaning beyond
absurdity. Let them be sure that every little deed
counts, that every word has power, and that we
can—every one—do our share to redeem the world
in spite of all absurdities and all frustrations and all
disappointments. And above all, remember that
the meaning of life is to build a life as if it were a
work of art.

—Rabbi Abraham Heschel
(quoted in Greenleaf, 1977)

Alone at home, trying to sleep in ninety-five-degree heat with no
air conditioning, Bill sensed the question stalking him like a starving pack of wolves. He had expressed faith in God for over fifteen
years. Yet as he looked back at his life, he saw little evidence that
anything supernatural had influenced the outcome. Thinking of his
job, his family, and his church activities, Bill wondered, "Can any
of this really be attributed to anything but my own efforts?"

Bill had been looking for the evidence of God's hand in the ex-
ternal things—career, ministry, and family success. Then it dawned
on him:

This isn't about what has been done. It's about *me*, isn't it? Could
God be asking me to trust him with my weaknesses? My destructive
habits? The things I don't let others see? Could God possibly turn
me into something good? I know I can't turn myself around. Maybe
God can.

Bill had tried many times to overcome the wounds of his past, some of them self-inflicted, but he could not get around them. Each time a significant opportunity arose, these old injuries and scars held him back. They kept him from emotional intimacy with his wife. They created a gap between him and his kids. They hurt his job performance and career choices. They even distanced Bill from those he longed to reach out and help—the hippies and street kids of the early 1970s.

Could God be asking me to trust him with my weaknesses? My destructive habits? The things I don't let others see?

That restless night marked a turning point. Bill asked God to turn his life into far more than he could make it on his own by dealing with the issues of his heart that affected his character and influence. For the first time in a long time, Bill chose humble vulnerability over self-protective defense. He could not have known how his destiny was being shaped that night. And he could not have known how one evening of conviction and faith would be tested over and over again.

Two years later, Bill flew to Los Angeles to meet with the managing partner of the accounting firm he worked for. Over lunch, this very distinguished gentleman presented Bill with the opportunity to begin the process of becoming a partner. Bill truly appreciated the offer but said he and his wife could not decide until January— three months later.

The following Monday, a political friend called Bill from Washington. "Barry Goldwater is here with me. We'd like you to come to Washington to work as part of the Arizona delegation of the Republican Party."

Again, Bill answered, "Thank you. I'm honored. This sounds like an incredible opportunity. But I'm afraid I can't let you know until January. My wife and I . . ."

"What?" the friend responded. "Bill, do you realize what this could lead to?"

Bill could hear Goldwater saying some choice words in the background. Neither his friend nor Goldwater took Bill's response very well: "As I was saying, Grace and I are trying to decide what we should pursue during the next season of our lives. I'm not ruling it out. I'm just saying I need until January."

The following Tuesday, the president of Bill's alma mater called. "Would you consider coming back here in a significant leadership role?"

Bill responded the same way.

Three weeks. Three opportunities. Which should he pursue? Accounting? Politics? Education? All strongly appealed to Bill. All offered a significant leadership role, congruent with his strengths and calling. All possessed inherent risks, including the fact that choosing one meant rejecting the others. And what if he chose the wrong one? He and Grace had about two months left to make up their minds.

By January, they had rejected all three options and had chosen a fourth that offered no stability, little or no pay, and no prestige or political power. But it aligned with the desire of their hearts and what they believed to be God's desire for their lives. It gave them the opportunity to love and teach truth to a group of hippies and street kids. For nearly thirty years now, they have invested their lives in these "fringe" people and countless others and have received tremendous returns on those investments. The process has unearthed many of the principles you've read in this book—and much more.

Worthwhile Choices

Was it the right choice? Bill and Grace think so, and so do many people they have influenced. Broken men and women have been healed and have entered into successful careers, some winning honors for their valued contributions. Marriages have been restored, even after years of divorce. Bill has watched alcoholics and drug addicts come clean and victims of child abuse become capable of loving others. People in pain have become successful business owners, teachers, medical professionals, pastors, and participants in other vocations too numerous to mention. But all shared a common bond. Each found hope, healing, acceptance, and love in a community that honored them for who they really were and affirmed their unique calling and contribution to the world. All of this occurred, not because of Bill and Grace's superior talents or those of their teams but because they chose the character ladder.

As Bill allowed God and others to see and touch the issues of his heart, he developed genuine humility—the kind nobody brags about. In humility, he gained the trust to choose vulnerability, allowing God and trusted friends to speak truth to him, even to the deepest, darkest parts of his life. Bill also gained the trust he needed to align with truth, submitting to the love of others. As he did, instead of viewing himself as the neglected, abandoned son of alcoholic parents, a new Bill began to emerge from the wreckage.

The old Bill rejected love because of his own flawed perceptions of himself. But the newly emerging Bill could receive love and give love. The old Bill couldn't let truth penetrate his heart and could only teach the words of truth to others. The new Bill could receive truth and transfer it into the lives of others.

Bill's motives began to change as the radical transformation took place, and, in turn, so did his values and actions. Whereas the old Bill could do a lot, the new Bill could really be somebody he and others respected—who, incidentally, could still do a lot.

Looking back, Bill and those who know him can see something beyond the seemingly illogical challenges and joys of the last twenty-five years. They see a work of art from the hands of a master, crafting spatters and splotches, dark colors and vibrant colors, into a painting that only God could produce. Bill can look back and say, "Yes, God did that," because he knows beyond a doubt that he couldn't have done it himself. He couldn't even fix an air conditioner one very hot, summer evening.

Mastering the Tools

Like Bill, each of us is a work of art in progress, with the responsibility of participating in the process. What we become is the result of a collaborative effort. We must learn to master some of the same tools God uses. A painter has brushes, oils, and canvas. To develop character, we must develop relationships and infuse our environments with grace. We must choose the path of trust, vulnerability, and obedience. But reading about these tools, as you have in this book, cannot make you a master any more than reading about painting will make you a great painter. To become a painter, you must start painting. To develop character, you must begin to try out the principles of developing character.

The Context of Community

Begin with community. Community happens one relationship at a time; therefore it is never beyond your grasp. You will begin to see what you can truly accomplish when you find friendships in which you can explore inner needs and strengths. So how do you start?

Find allies who are willing to stand with you. Most great movements in art—and most other fields for that matter—came about when people with similar passions and goals came together to support one another. You can do the same. They may not be people whom you trust entirely at first, but they should be people whom you are willing to have earn and keep your trust. They may be peers, teachers, coworkers, superiors, or subordinates. You need people who will tell you the truth and who will also receive truth from you without risk of jeopardizing the friendship.

You also need people who are willing to have fun and laugh with you. One of the most powerful gifts of grace is its permission to laugh and enjoy, just for the sake of its delight. Its unguarded play-fulness promises anyone who gets close that here there is safety, respect, joy, and deep appreciation. Productivity and creative, play-ful fun and laughter play off each other in a beautiful and significant way. Few marks of a healthy culture are as easily received and entered into as trust-engendered laughter.

Take Time to Practice

If you wanted to become a great artist, it would require practice, practice, and more practice. You would have to rework and revise and polish and perfect your work in the face of apathy and adver-sity. Neil Simon rewrote his first play, "Come Blow Your Horn," thirty-three times before it opened on Broadway. During the first act of the opening, a patron in the balcony died. Undeterred, Simon went on to become one of America's most successful playwrights.

To develop trusted relationships in which character can be de-veloped, you must commit time and effort to the process. It may mean a weekly or monthly meeting with another person or group. The best environments are produced when a core group commits themselves to each other for life, no matter what. Such a commit-ment may be hard for some to make, but even committing for a def-inite period of time works wonders.

With such time commitments, people feel more free to let down their guard. Without them, vulnerability becomes very difficult. When someone commits to us for life (as in a marriage), that com-mitment helps us gain the security and freedom we need to be who we really are. Committing time creates opportunities for vulnera-bility. Vulnerability builds trust. And sooner than we think, we will be able to encourage one another on the character ladder.

Hitting Snags

As you begin to experience the stuff of life together in community, you will begin to notice the true strengths you and others possess. You'll also discover flaws and weaknesses.

When you try to create an environment in which the deeper aspects of strengths and weaknesses can be addressed, a whole squid-tank full of reactions come out. It's much like introducing truth into a dysfunctional family. When an addict faces the truth and gets well, everyone related to the addict begins to realize how out of whack they had become in their efforts to adapt to the addict's behavior. Some acknowledge their codependence. Others face their own attempts at denial or escape. The only way for systemic, healthy change to occur is when all those in the system face the truth and realign with the new reality.

We've seen this dynamic rather clearly close up. At one of our training conferences, an executive team began to explore the character-ladder process, thinking they had little to learn. Most had been friends for years. But about halfway through, their senior leader revealed that his team really didn't know him at all. He had been struggling for years with increasing isolation and guilt over his inability to perform in certain areas. But he didn't feel he had the freedom to tell them the truth.

At first his team felt shocked. Then they felt regret at how their assumptions had hurt their teammate and leader. They determined to change their habits to align with truth rather than with false assumptions, committing themselves to authentic community. Within a few months, what they learned from each other began to have an impact on their organization as they redesigned their roles around who they really were rather than according to past assumptions reinforced by years of organizational history.

Another team had a different experience. Uncomfortable from the outset, they fought the process tooth and nail. Eventually, they accepted the fact that even though they worked together every day they simply did not know each other. They didn't trust each another and especially did not trust their senior leader. They responded to the truth as if it were a bumblebee in their car; some tried to kill it, while others simply jumped out of the moving vehicle. The process led them into increasing pain until, months later, several of the team members resigned, convinced they could not live in an environment where their teammates and leaders neglected the rungs and rails of the character ladder.

Will you move toward trust, vulnerability, truth, and integrity? Or will you pull back like a homeowner closing the door on a vacuum cleaner salesman? Make no mistake about it: community is the context for the development of character. It is the only context for going above and beyond our individual best, for developing extraordinary character and influence. Getting started is as simple as sticking your neck out and communicating trust to the person in the next apartment, house, cubicle, office, or pew.

Thy Will Be Done

God's plan could mean stepping up to a challenge. *It could mean stepping down.* But each step brings us closer to our destiny if it leads to greater love for God and others. Whether our sphere of influence is small or large, the possibilities for personal growth remain the same. We can watch our motives transform from selfishness to selflessness. We can submit to the Master's loving hand, becoming what we need to become for the benefit of others and our world.

A few years ago at the Seattle Special Olympics, nine contestants, all physically or mentally disabled, assembled at the starting line for the hundred-yard dash. At the gun, they all started out, not exactly in a dash but with a relish to run the race to the finish and win. All, that is, except one little boy, who stumbled on the asphalt, tumbled over a couple of times, and began to cry. The other eight heard the boy cry. They slowed down, paused, and looked back. Then they all turned around and went back. Every one of them. One girl with Down's syndrome bent over, kissed him, and said, "This will make it better." Then all nine linked arms and walked together to the finish line. Everyone in the stadium stood, and the cheering went on for several minutes.[1]

This story has been retold countless times. Why? Because hearing about ordinary people doing extraordinary things strikes a chord in our souls. Deep down we know that helping others matters far more than winning a hollow victory for ourselves. But like those disabled children, changing our course requires us to pause and hear the cries of others. Changing our course also requires us to pause and listen to the cry within our own hearts.

What we do matters less than who we are. How we do things matters less than for whom we do them. Who we become and who we serve will reveal whether we are climbing both ladders or relying solely on our capacities. The rails and rungs we choose will determine the destiny we find and the legacy we leave.

What we do matters less than who we are. How we do things matters less than for whom we do them.

A woman once had a dream in which she wandered into a shop at the mall and found Jesus behind a counter. "You can have anything your heart desires," Jesus said to her. Astounded but pleased, she asked for peace, love, happiness, wisdom, and freedom from fear. Then she added, "Not just for me, but for the whole earth."

Jesus smiled and said, "I think you misunderstand me. We don't sell fruits, only seeds."[2]

For our sake and for the sakes of our children and grand-children, we need to take the first step now. The seed of destiny within each of us was put there to bear fruit in the lives of others. It awaits the fertile soil of community and an environment of grace.

When Jesus walked this earth, in every city, in every backwater town, he cried out in a variety of ways, *"Is anyone thirsty?"* Most who heard him went about their business, ignoring or mocking this stranger with his odd band of misfits. But some heard his words and drew near. Not because they were noble or wise or discerning or religious. *They were just so very, very thirsty.* They were so very tired of bluffing adequacy, of pretending competency, of trying to limp through the day-to-day, alone. And here was someone claiming to have the cooling water—the longed-for help—they craved.

And so here we are, modern-day bluffing limpers, thirsty and tired, coming to the end of a book promising water. And we are afraid. Because hucksters are as common as pocket lint. And we are afraid because even though the ladder we had been climbing wasn't getting us to where we so desperately longed to go, at least it *looked* nice. And we are frightened because we are not sure that we can go back to a capacity-only ladder. Because we have seen that the emperor who thought he was so regally dressed is naked for all to see. But we are frightened of this new ladder because we feel all alone on this journey into the unknown.

Well, look around you, weary one. You'll see a whole bunch of us standing next to you who are thirsty, too. We've got your back. We've stepped on the ladder, as you have, and we can't step off now. The cost is too high. It would mean going back to a cold land, where we have to bluff our worth again around others who have to bluff theirs behind thin, quivering smiles. No, that conspiracy of frightened, hidden silence ends here. There is another way. We know too much now. There is a place *beyond your best*. And the dream will never stop nagging us if we don't try it out. There's too much on the line. Friends are watching us; kids are watching us to see what we'll do. There ain't no going back. This life is too short for vanity. Step on up. This ladder will hold.

Grabbing Hold

- Whom do you trust with you? Whom are you willing to trust with you?
- What benefits of selflessness and interdependence can you list? How can you become selfless and interdependent?
- Who are your allies in your climb up the character ladder? Where can you find more allies?
- Where will you begin to build a community of grace? How will it be sustained?

Notes

Introduction

1. Peterson, 1993, pp. 53, 112. Also see Matthew 18:4 and Mark 10:15.

Chapter One

1. Behe, 1912. The words of Smith and the crew were recounted from survivors of the wreck and probably represent a synthesis of several accounts. The Website listed in the References provides excellent analysis and eyewitness reports from the *Titanic* and many different views of Captain Smith's final moments. But as the official board of inquiry decided, Captain Smith ultimately was responsible for the catastrophe. Whether others prodded him to make such decisions has no bearing on his responsibility to evaluate his options and act with good judgment.

Chapter Two

1. Barry, 2002.
2. Schultz, 2002. The Charles Schultz Philosophy can be found at www.shameno.com/daily/archive/020925charles.htm.
3. See Genesis 1–3, especially Genesis 1:28.
4. Pascal. This quote can be found at www.a-voice.org/xtras/xo56.htm.

Chapter Three

1. Hugo, 1961, pp. 17–25, 32–33.
2. Lamott, 1999, p. 134.
3. May, 1988, p. 173.
4. Argyris, 1962, p. 43.
5. Pinsky, 2001, pp. 65, 72.
6. McEachern, 1998.

Chapter Four

1. This story can be found at www.cyberstory.com/ CyberStoryText2/Sandpiper.html.
2. See Revelation 3:14, 17; Proverbs 3:5–6; John 15:1–7; and 1 Corinthians 12:20–21 and 16:14.
3. Lewis, 1946, pp. 18–19.
4. Sanders, 2002, p. 64.
5. Willingham, 1997, p. 76.
6. Source unknown.

Chapter Five

1. See John 12:24.
2. Barry, 1989, pp. 199–200.
3. Blanchard, Oster, and Hamel, forthcoming in April 2003.
4. 1 Peter 5:6.
5. See, for example, Romans 8.
6. See Genesis 20.

Chapter Six

1. Hendricks, 1994. This was said during his plenary address at the Leadership Forum.
2. McCourt, 1998, pp. 71–72.

Chapter Seven

1. Bonger, 1998. The information on Vincent van Gogh's life came primarily from his own letters to his brother Theo and the memoirs of his sister-in-law, Jo van Gogh Bonger. Both can be found on the Website dedicated to Vincent's life and work: http://van-gogh.org.
2. Ibid.
3. Buechner, 1996, p. 139.

Chapter Eight

1. Miller, 1997, audio book.
2. Brilliant, 1991.
3. Quoted in Ziglar, 1997, p. 80.
4. Peterson, 1993, p. 489.
5. Ibid.
6. Ibid.
7. See Luke 19:5–9.
8. See Mark 10:17–22.
9. See, for example, Proverbs 3:34 and 1 Peter 5:6.

Chapter Nine

1. Palmer, 2000, p. 44ff.
2. This biographical information was compiled from two sources: Gonzalez-Balado and Playfoot, 1985, and Chawla, 1992.
3. This biographical information was compiled from two sources: Mosley, 1982, and Cray, 1990.
4. Mackay, 1996, p. 178.
5. Psalm 75:6–7.
6. Luke 18:14.
7. 1 Peter 5:6.
8. Peck, 1993, p. 268.
9. Levoy, 1997, pp. 272–274.

Chapter Ten

1. Author unknown. One variation of this story can be found in Canfield and Hansen, 1993. Another can be found in Berke, 1998.
2. Adapted from De Mello, 1988, p. 103.

References

Argyris, C. *Interpersonal Competence and Organizational Effectiveness*. Homewood, Ill.: Dorsey Press and Irwin, 1962.

Barry, D. *Claw Your Way to the Top: How to Become the Head of a Major Corporation in Roughly a Week*. Emmaus, Pa.: Rodale Press, 1986.

Barry, D. *Dave Barry's Greatest Hits*. New York: Ballantine, 1989.

Barry, D. *The Dave Barry 2003 Block Calendar: America's Pulitzer Prize-Winning Humorist*. Kansas City, Mo.: Andrews McMeel, 2002.

Behe, G. *Titanic Tidbits*. London: (n.p.). [http://www.fortunecity.com/millenium/tulip/129/tree2.html]. Oct. 1998. (Originally published 1912.)

Berke, D. "The Spiritual Vision of Interfaith Fellowship: Basic Tenets." *On Course*. [http://www.interfaithfellowship.org/oncourse/articles/berke/berke6.html]. May–June 1998.

Blanchard, K., Oster, M., and Hamel, M. *Giving Back, Using Your Influence to Create Social Change*. Colorado Springs, Colo.: NavPress, forthcoming.

Bonger, J. "Selections from the Memoirs of Jo van Gogh Bonger." [http://van-gogh.org/docs/memoirs/memoirs]. Oct. 1998.

Briggs, D. "Protestants Still Fill Elite Ranks." *Arizona Republic*, Dec. 16, 1994, p. A22.

Brilliant, A. *I Have Abandoned My Search for Truth, and Am Now Looking for a Good Fantasy*. Santa Barbara, Calif.: Woodbridge Press, 1991.

Buechner, F. *The Longing for Home*. New York: HarperCollins, 1996.

Buford, B. *Half Time: Changing Your Game Plan from Success to Significance*. Grand Rapids, Mich.: Zondervan, 1994.

Canfield, J., and Hansen, M. V. *Chicken Soup for the Soul: 101 Stories to Open the Heart and Rekindle the Spirit*. Deerfield Beach, Fla.: Health Communications, 1993.

Chawla, N. *Mother Teresa: The Authorized Biography*. Rockport, Mass.: Element, 1992.

Clinton, J. R. *The Making of a Leader*. Colorado Springs, Colo.: NavPress, 1988.

Clinton, J. R. *Leadership in the Nineties: Six Factors to Consider*. Altadena, Calif.: Barnabas, 1992.

Clinton, J. R. *Focused Lives: Inspirational Life-Changing Lessons from Eight Effective Christian Leaders Who Finished Well*. Altadena, Calif.: Barnabas, 1995.

Colson, C., and Eckerd, J. *Why America Doesn't Work*. Dallas: Word, 1991.

Covey, S. *The Seven Habits of Highly Effective People*. New York: Simon & Schuster, 1989.

Cray, E. *General of the Army: George C. Marshall, Soldier and Statesman*. New York: W. W. Norton, 1990.

De Crescenzo, L. *Thus Spake Bellavista*. (A. Bardoni, trans.). New York: Grove Press, 1989.

De Mello, A. *Song of the Bird*. New York: Image Books, 1984.

De Mello, A. *Taking Flight: A Book of Story Meditations*. New York: Doubleday, 1988.

De Pree, M. *Leadership Is an Art*. New York: Dell, 1989.

De Pree, M. *Leading Without Power: Finding Hope in Serving Community*. San Francisco: Jossey-Bass, 1997.

De Saint-Exupéry, A. *The Wisdom of the Sands*. (S. Gilbert, trans.). Orlando: Harcourt Brace, 1950.

Farrar, S. *Finishing Strong: Finding the Power to Go the Distance*. Sisters, Oreg.: Multnomah, 1995.

Friess, F. Speech presented at a community leadership breakfast, Pinnacle Forum, Scottsdale, Ariz., Apr. 10, 1998.

Gonzalez-Balado, J. L., and Playfoot, J. N. (eds.). *My Life for the Poor: Mother Teresa of Calcutta*. San Francisco: HarperSanFrancisco, 1985.

Greenleaf, R. K. *Servant Leadership: A Journey into the Nature of Legitimate Power and Greatness*. Mahwah, N.J.: Paulist Press, 1977.

Hagberg, J. O. *Real Power: Stages of Personal Power in Organizations*. Salem, Wis.: Sheffield, 1994.

Harter, J. (ed.). *Thoughts on Success: Thoughts and Reflections from History's Great Thinkers*. Mineola, N.Y.: Dover, Forbes Subscriber Edition, 1995.

Hawken, P. *Growing a Business*. New York: Simon & Schuster, 1987.

Hendricks, H. "Plenary Address." Leadership Forum, Estes Park, Colo., 1994.

Hersey, P., and Blanchard, K. H. *Management of Organizational Behavior: Utilizing Human Resources*. (2nd ed.) Upper Saddle River, N.J.: Prentice Hall, 1992.

Hesselbein, F., Goldsmith, M., Beckhard, R., and Schubert, R. (eds.). *The Community of the Future*. San Francisco: Jossey-Bass, 1998.

Hugo, V. *Les Miserables*. (C. E. Wilbour, trans.; abridged by J. K. Robinson). New York: Fawcett Premier, 1961.

Jackson, M. "Bosses Held in Low Esteem and Sinking Fast, Study Says: Anger, Skepticism Fill Workplace, Survey Finds." *Arizona Republic*, Sept. 2, 1997, p. E1.

James, W. *Principles of Psychology*. New York: Dover, 1979. (Originally published 1890.)

Jaworski, J. *Synchronicity: The Inner Path of Leadership*. San Francisco: Berrett-Koehler, 1996.

Kierkegaard, S. *Journal 1848*. (H. V. Hong and E. H. Hong, eds.). Bloomington: Indiana University Press, 1848.

Kouzes, J. M., and Posner, B. Z. *The Leadership Challenge: How to Get Extraordinary Things Done in Organizations*. San Francisco: Jossey-Bass, 1987.

Kouzes, J. M., and Posner, B. Z. *Encouraging the Heart: A Leader's Guide to Rewarding and Recognizing Others*. San Francisco: Jossey-Bass, 1999.

Kuhn, M. *Get Out There and Do Something About Injustice*. New York: Friendship Press, 1972.

Kurtz, E., and Ketcham, K. *The Spirituality of Imperfection: Storytelling and the Journey to Wholeness*. New York: Bantam Books, 1992.

Lamott, A. *Traveling Mercies*. New York: Pantheon Books, 1999.

Leifer, S. "Entrepreneurs' Forum in Hale Boasts a Stellar Lineup." [http://www.bus.umich.edu/news/hale.html]. Oct. 6, 1997.

Levoy, G. *CALLINGS: Finding and Following an Authentic Life*. New York: Harmony Books, 1997.

Lewis, C. S. *The Great Divorce*. New York: HarperCollins, 1946.

Mackay, H. *Swim with the Sharks Without Being Eaten Alive: Outsell, Outmanage, Outmotivate, and Outnegotiate Your Competition*. New York: Fawcett Books, 1996.

May, G. G. *Addiction and Grace: Love and Spirituality in the Healing of Addictions*. New York: HarperCollins, 1988.

McCourt, M. *A Monk Swimming*. New York: Hyperion, 1998.

McEachern, R. Speech presented at Apple Computer, Cupertino, Calif., Dec. 1998.

McManus, P., and Holt, H. *They Shoot Canoes Don't They?* New York: Henry Holt, 1982.

Miller, D. *The Rants*. New York: Doubleday, 1997.

Mosley, L. *Marshall: Hero for Our Times*. New York: Hearst, 1982.

Nash, B. M., and Zullo, A. *The Misfortune 500: Featuring the Business Hall of Shame*. New York: Pocket Books, 1988.

Newport, F., and Saad, L. "Religious Faith Is Widespread but Many Skip Church." Gallup Poll Archives, 1997. [http://198.175.140.8/ POLL_ARCHIVES/1997/970329.htm]. Oct. 1998.

"No Room at the Top? How a Big Five Accounting Firm Changed Its Culture to Support Women." CNNfn. [http://cnnfn.com/fortune/9903/04/fortune_deloitte/]. Mar. 4, 1999.

Norris, K. *Hands Full of Living*. Mattituck, N.Y.: Amereon, 1988.

Palmer, P. *Let Your Life Speak* (condensed). San Francisco: Jossey-Bass, 2000.

Pascal, B. "Moral Extras." [http://www.a-voice.org/xtras/x056.htm]. Dec. 17, 2002.

Peck, M. S. *A World Waiting to Be Born: Civility Rediscovered*. New York: Bantam Books, 1993.

Peterson, E. H. *The Message: The New Testament in Contemporary Language*. Colorado Springs, Colo.: NavPress, 1993.

Pinsky, M. *The Gospel According to the Simpsons*. Louisville, Ky.: Westminster John Knox Press, 2001.

Pollard, C. W. *The Soul of the Firm*. Grand Rapids, Mich.: Zondervan, 1996.

Prolificus. "Quotes About Wisdom." [http://www.prolificus.com/commongenius/wisdom.html]. May 11, 1999.

Rawson, H. *Unwritten Laws: The Unofficial Rules of Life*. New York: Crown, 1997.

Redmoon, A. "No Peaceful Warriors." *Gnosis*. Fall, 1991.

Rookmaaker, H. R. *Art Needs No Justification*. Downers Grove, Ill.: InterVarsity Press, 1978.

Rubin, H. "Peter's Principles." *Inc.*, Mar. 1, 1998.

Rudner, R. *Naked Beneath My Clothes: Tales of a Revealing Nature*. New York: Penguin, 1992.

Saad, L. "'Most Admired' Poll Finds Americans Lack Major Heroes: Mother Teresa's Death Leaves a Void on List of Most Admired Women." Gallup Poll Archives, 1998. [http://198.175.140.8/POLL_ARCHIVES/980101.htm].

Sadeh, P. *Jewish Folktales*. (H. Halkin, trans.). New York: Doubleday, 1989.

Sanders, T. "Love Is the Killer App." *Fast Company*, Feb, 2002, p. 64.

Schaef, A. W., and Fassel, D. *The Addictive Organization: Why We Overwork, Cover Up, Pick Up the Pieces, Please the Boss and Perpetuate Sick Organizations*. San Francisco: HarperSanFrancisco, 1988.

Schein, E. H. *Organizational Culture and Leadership*. San Francisco: Jossey-Bass, 1985.

Schultz, C. "The Charles Schultz Philosophy." [http://www.shemano.com/daily/archive/020925charles.html]. Sept. 25, 2002.

Schultz, H., and Yang, D. J. *Pour Your Heart into It: How Starbucks Built a Company One Cup at a Time*. New York: Hyperion, 1999.

Senge, P., Kleiner, A., Roberts, C., Ross, R., and Smith, B. *The Fifth Discipline Fieldbook*. New York: Doubleday, 1994.

Shaw, R. B. *Trust in the Balance: Building Successful Organizations on Results, Integrity, and Concern*. San Francisco: Jossey-Bass, 1997.

Steindl-Rast, D., and Lebell, S. *The Music of Silence: Entering the Sacred Space of Monastic Experience*. (Sound recording). Los Angeles: Audio Renaissance Tapes, 1995.

Stephanopoulos, G. *All Too Human: A Political Education*. Boston: Little, Brown, 1999.

Taff, R., Taff, T., and Hollihan, J. "Healing Touch." In *Russ Taff*. (Sound recording). Waco, Tex.: Word Records, 1987.

Teresa, M. *A Simple Path*. New York: Ballantine Books, 1995.

Thoreau, H. D. *Walden*. [http://www2.cybernex.net/~rlenat/walden00.html]. (Originally published 1854.)

Toney, F., and Oster, M. *The Leader and Religious Faith: The Relationship Between the Exercise of Religious Faith by CEOs and Goal Achievement, Self-Fulfillment, and Social Benefits.* Self-published study, 1997.

Whyte, D. *The Heart Aroused: Poetry and the Preservation of the Soul in Corporate America.* New York: Doubleday, 1994.

Willard, D. *The Spirit of the Disciplines.* New York: HarperCollins, 1988.

Willingham, R. *The People Principle: A Revolutionary Redefinition of Leadership.* New York: St. Martin's Press, 1997.

Yancy, P. *Church: Why Bother? My Personal Pilgrimage.* Grand Rapids, Mich.: Zondervan, 1998.

Ziglar, Z. *Over the Top.* Nashville, Tenn.: Thomas Nelson, 1997.

Zimmerman, M. E. *Eclipse of the Self.* Athens: Ohio University Press, 1981.

The Authors

Bill Thrall serves as leadership mentor for Leadership Catalyst, Inc., a nonprofit organization dedicated to building and restoring trust in leaders and the people they influence. Prior to Leadership Catalyst, Bill led Open Door Fellowship in Phoenix, a church he founded in 1973. His discerning wisdom, forged in the trenches of pastoring others for three decades, provides rich benefits to many boards and leaders in various countries. Before his involvement in vocational ministry, Bill was a CPA and management consultant. Bill and his wife, Grace, have three married children—Bill, Wende, and Joy—and seven grandchildren.

Bruce McNicol is the visionary founder-president of Leadership Catalyst. Bruce applies international experience and degrees in finance/law, leadership development, and theology to help leaders create environments where people can journey beyond their best. From 1985 to 1995, Bruce served as president of Interest Associates, based in Chicago, Illinois. In that role, he empowered innovative urban partnerships and guided leaders from twelve cultures to establish over a hundred churches and organizations throughout North America. He is married to Janet, who is a homemaker and nurse. They have three children—Nicole, Chad, and Ryan.

Ken McElrath has a dual passion. An artist at heart, he is always creating. Whether crafting organizational change, remodeling his home, or dabbling with an oil painting, he thrives on challenging the status quo. He also aspires to see creativity permeate the lives of leaders and the cultures they impact. Ken leads CAZABBA, a marketing and creative services company. Prior to this, Ken held several senior marketing positions with Fortune 500, startup technology, software, retail services, and training companies, including Leadership Catalyst. Ken and his wife, Donna, live in Phoenix and are raising three children—Zach, Tommy, and Anne.

Leadership Catalyst

One word has the power to catalyze greatness in an individual, an organization, or a nation: *Trust*. Surveys show that trust is the #1 requirement for success in life and leadership. But for many, trust has been hard to come by or misplaced. There is a painful Trust Gap . . . and it appears to be widening in many arenas of business, education, government, church, and even family life.

The *mission* of Leadership Catalyst is to build and restore *trust* in leaders and in those they influence. Established in 1995, Leadership Catalyst is recognized as an international resource for helping leaders learn how to develop trust and authentic environments of character, vision, and productivity.

For the *individual*, Leadership Catalyst offers a variety of resource tools to help you build trust in your friendships, your family, and your community.

For the *organization*, Leadership Catalyst has designed a groundbreaking process to help leaders and teams bridge the Trust Gap. Delivery of the learning process is implemented through your organization's coaches, who are trained in Catalyst Coaches' Clinics.

For additional information on Leadership Catalyst and our latest resource catalog, please contact us directly:

Leadership Catalyst, Inc.
1600 E. Northern Ave, Suite 280
Phoenix, AZ 85020
Voice: 602–249–7000 (Phoenix area)
Voice: 888–249–0700 (Toll-free in North America)
Fax: 602–249–0611
Email: info@leadershipcatalyst.org
Website: www.leadershipcatalyst.org